MORE THAN 220 RECIPES FROM THE HUDSON VALLEY

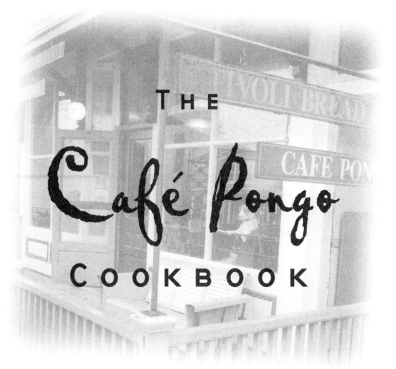

The Café Pongo COOKBOOK

VALERIE NEHEZ

Photographs by Joseph M. Schram

SIMON & SCHUSTER

NEW YORK LONDON TORONTO SYDNEY SINGAPORE

SIMON & SCHUSTER
Rockefeller Center
1230 Avenue of the Americas
New York, NY 10020

SIMON & SCHUSTER and colophon are registered trademarks
of Simon & Schuster, Inc.

Designed by Karolina Harris

Manufactured in the United States of America

10   9   8   7   6   5   4   3   2   1

Library of Congress Cataloging-in-Publication Data
Nehez, Valerie.
    The Café Pongo Cookbook : more than 220 recipes from the Hudson Valley /
Valerie Nehez ; photographs by Joseph M. Schram.
        p.   cm.
    Includes index.
    1. Cookery, American.   2. Cookery—Hudson River Valley (N.Y. and N.J.)
3. Café Pongo.   I. Title.
TX715.N388 2001
641.5973—dc21   2001041164

ISBN 0-684-87137-8

Contents

2. Soups   63

3. Salads and Sandwiches   89

4. Starters and Small Dishes   115

5. Entrées 145

INTRODUCTION

the past fifteen years I have owned a restaurant in New York's Hudson River Valley. During the restaurant's off-season I travel. I have been through all of Central America. I have visited South America, Thailand, Laos, Europe, Africa, and many islands in the Caribbean. I have stayed in hundreds of hotels and eaten in thousands of restaurants. Every time I go on a trip, no matter where, eventually a strong desire to return to the Hudson Valley sets in. When I am home and I'm rushing to pick up new blades for the exhaust fan, or some other trivial errand, I speed over the Kingston-Rhinecliff Bridge and see nothing. But when I cross that same bridge on my way back from the airport, I see a Frederic Church painting; I see the Tivoli water tower; I see our tiny brick train station; I see all the way from Germantown to Saugerties.

I was drawn to the Hudson River Valley for the gourmet eating and the ethereal setting, but my interest in food and cooking began at a much earlier age.

I grew up in Philadelphia and spent summers with my grandmother in Merchantville, New Jersey. There was always a stock or spaghetti sauce with beef or venison bones simmering very low on her stove. We picked Jersey beefsteak tomatoes in her garden and made tomato sandwiches. We picked mulberries from her tree and made pies. And then we relaxed and ate dinner on TV trays while watching Lawrence Welk at 7:30.

My mother did not share her mother's enthusiasm for cooking, so as the self-appointed family chef, I fine-tuned my culinary skills. At age seven, I and my best friend, Julie Levinson, often mixed ingredients completely at random, cooked them, and attempted to trick someone into eating the results. Our most successful venture was a seeded cake. It was made with birdseed.

Much to my parents' disappointment, I often overlooked the homework assigned at my private school to work at my minimum-wage job at Roy Rogers. I had priorities: I loved to operate the soft-serve ice-cream machine, and I was the large-fry sales champion in my district.

Back at home, my first signature dish was baked chicken made with Catalina dressing, dry onion soup mix, and apricot jam. My first business venture was at my grade-school fair. I loved Pennsylvania Dutch funnel cakes, so I volunteered my friends and set up a booth. With a bunch of electric skillets, we were in business. We were cranking out funnel cakes like pros on an assembly line until we ran out of oil—my first lesson in inventory. In 1984, at age nineteen, I enrolled at Bard College in upstate New York, three miles south of the town of Tivoli. At age twenty I left college and started a restaurant.

On my first drive through Tivoli, I saw a shell of a former town. I saw many turn-of-the-century storefronts, either boarded up or with Indian tapestries tacked over the windows in an effort to turn them into apartments. The buildings had charming architectural details still intact. Stopping the car and peeking through dusty windows, I could see high tin ceilings through the original glass of the storefront windows. The only people I saw that day were two old men who had set up camp at the corner sitting on a carpeted stoop with a small American flag. The only business that appeared to be open was a laundromat. Having not brought laundry, I stayed in the car.

At a yard sale, I found a paperback history of Tivoli, by Dick Wiles, a professor at Bard. The book's reprinted photographs of Tivoli's glory days testified to

the bustling past I had imagined. My affection for Tivoli grew as I learned more local history. Over the past fifteen years, I've collected a mental archive of Hudson Valley and Tivoli lore, from the myth of Rip Van Winkle to (perhaps no less mythical) tales of Eleanor Roosevelt tippling beers in Tivoli's Hotel Morey. Still referred to as *The Hotel* (despite not having rented rooms for half a century), the Morey claims to be the longest-running single-family-owned bar in the country. I've visited every single historic home open to the public and trespassed on many more abandoned properties that are not.

The Hudson River Valley is vast, but the little towns sprinkled just north and south of the Kingston-Rhinecliff Bridge are those that have become the most significant in my life. Rhinebeck and Rhinecliff, Barrytown, Annandale-on-Hudson, Saugerties, Clermont, Linlithgo, and, of course, Tivoli. The names have an incantatory power. Tivoli came into its own in the late nineteenth century. Before the bridges were built, steamships crossed the river, carrying workers from Tivoli to their jobs in the foundries directly across the river in Saugerties and then back again. Taverns and brothels flourished, as well as many stores and shops up and down Broadway. Eventually the local economy shifted, and the foundries closed. When bridges were built south of Tivoli, the ferries stopped running. By 1984, around the time of my first visit, Tivoli was silent.

I eventually rented one of those storefront apartments with Indian tapestries tacked over the windows. I moved in a threadbare sofa and called it home. The tapestries came down and the sofa was tossed. My partner and I built four tables and bought sixteen chairs from Kmart. We were in business, serving fresh Mexican dishes to locals and students. The menu consisted of only a few basic never-fail recipes. We called the place Santa Fe. It felt like "playing restaurant." When hip and dressy vacationing New Yorkers first came in, I worried that they would think that it wasn't a "real" restaurant and that the jig would be up. We had one set of four hand-painted matching pottery plates. I would get them out for the "fancy" guests and pray that a fifth person didn't appear as he or she would have to eat off paper, like everyone else.

The restaurant rapidly grew, nourished by glowing reviews from the local papers. The press, I think, couldn't help but be kind. We were so young and the location of the restaurant was considered to be the middle of nowhere. It was the great American underdog story. During the next few years those four tables blossomed into a 170-seat success story—a real restaurant, and the business that started the boom in Tivoli, New York. The evolution was the exciting part. After almost ten years of successful restaurant partnership, I felt I needed to prove that the first time wasn't dumb luck. I needed to see what I could do on my own. With all my saved capital, I bought another abandoned storefront building in Tivoli and decided to venture it alone. (Today, Tivoli's business district has 100 percent occupancy, including four popular after-hours spots and, most recently, a first-rate sushi bar.) Café Pongo was named after the world's sweetest spotted mutt. (I chose a dog's name because more than anything else, a dog makes me feel most at home.) Café Pongo arose out of a sincere desire to create lovely food with great attention to detail and serve it in a warm and intimate environment.

Opening Café Pongo was far more terrifying *because* the Santa Fe had been so successful. The first time we had nothing to lose; this time there were expectations. We started serving just breakfast and lunch along with baked goods and coffee. Later we added a dinner menu, a full bar, and eventually catering, too. No matter what the meal, I wanted every customer to have a flawless experience. I insisted that every single item be made, from start to finish, on the premises, despite the common wisdom that this would be my economic downfall. It is entirely possible to run a restaurant and bakery in which you never dirty a pot or a mixing bowl. It's easy these days to buy breads, pastries, and bagels that are all precooked. A restaurant or bakery can simply bake off or brown these frozen goodies and tell the customers that they're "baked on the premises." (In my opinion this is the practice of fakery, not bakery.) Once at a food show, I even saw an "instant paella" packet. The company provided the restaurant with fancy serving bowls, and all that was required was to mix this packet with boiling water and an entire paella would puff up, complete with mussels in shells! I refused to give up hand-shaped breads and brioche and soup made with real stock. It took years to explain to customers that we didn't sell bagels because we didn't bake bagels.

I quickly realized, however, that my holier-than-thou, all-from-scratch plan needed a staff of fifty to be executed properly. The simple menu at Santa Fe had been created because in the beginning there were only two of us to make everything. My new vision required a full-time pastry chef, a full-time saucier, a full-time line chef, and a dining-room manager. And who was going to drive around and pick up all the stuff from the sweet Ma and Pa farms that didn't have the manpower to make deliveries? There was so much charm and potential at Pongo, I knew that if I waited long enough the right *multi*talented people would come along to help make it work. Everyone had to do a little of everything until the restaurant became busy enough to support a larger staff. In the meantime, neighbors from Tivoli helped fill in the blank spots. They lent me old blenders when the food processor burned up, and seated people when I was cooking. Our original loyal following of customers waited far longer than they should have for food and drinks; yet people always seemed to appreciate the integrity and feel of the experience.

Cassandra Purdy was the first person to really help me get Pongo into shape. She and I wore quite a few hats. Cassy drove an hour to work in a rickety old Volvo that often required her to stop and make on-the-spot repairs. I remain impressed that she could both fix her car *and* bake. She started work at 3:00 A.M. and never missed a shift. Once I changed the lock and forgot to give her a new key; she just jimmied open a window and started work on time. Cassy's spirit is responsible for the core of all the pastries and desserts at Pongo. Even though she had to leave after only two years, she trained Michael "Mikee" Gonella (the only other baker we've ever had). She has been instrumental in helping me write this book, driving from Connecticut once a week to test recipes with me. I always ask her, "Does this taste good?" Thankfully, she usually smiles and assures me, "It tastes really good."

In the four years since it opened, Café Pongo had grown. The café was open six days a week for breakfast, lunch, and dinner. After hours, at the bar, we started bringing in live music, which was well received and quite popular. During the summer season we were catering at least one event every weekend. Pongo had grown into many viable businesses under the same roof, and we still needed to find the other essential people. I was still in charge of the kitchen, bar, inventory, dining room, and ever-growing catering business. The good news was that the catering business was flourishing; the bad news was that the restaurant was suffering as a result. One night I came back from catering a film shoot with Gena Rowlands and Brooke Shields. The event was a great success; I'd received hugs and praise only to return to the restaurant and find that (a) it had been really busy; (b) the dishwasher hadn't shown up; (c) the chef had to leave because her tattooed and toothless boyfriend was in a car accident; and (d) the manager, who'd been washing dishes and cooking all night, had suddenly decided to go back to school. I needed someone else to run this business that was expanding faster than my ability to manage it. Enter Roland.

Walter Roland Butler, an old college friend, became the chef and now operates Café Pongo. He brought with him fifteen years of cooking experience, as well as a tremendous amount of pure talent. He says the secret to his success is starting each day with "a good strong cup of knowing what the hell I'm doing." In addition to becoming a world-class baker, Mikee has kept Pongo together by repairing every piece of equipment in the building, his only tool being a butter knife, while not burning the sticky buns.

We three are the core of this large and diversified business. Roland runs the restaurant. I am in charge of all off-premise catered events and promotions including food writing and creating this book. Mikee manages all of Pongo's wholesale baking accounts and supervises all the baking for catered events and the café. We have all worked hard to maintain the purity and integrity of our food and the environment in which that food is served. Being in the Hudson River Valley, surrounded by dairy farms, sheep farms, poultry farms, fruit orchards, and vegetable and herb growers, makes our job a lot easier than it might be elsewhere. (I admit, though, that I don't always want to know the given name of the lamb we're serving.) We fight to preserve a certain integrity in our business and in our food, but it's an integrity untainted by saccharine insincerity.

In 1984 Tivoli was boarded up, abandoned, and forgotten. Now every storefront on Broadway, Tivoli's main street, hums with activity. I was one of two original businesspeople who, bucking doubt and sage advice, decided to invest time and money in the village. Looking out from the windows of Pongo on a busy Friday and seeing Tivoli's sidewalks alive with people, I feel a tremendous sense of pride and accomplishment. The life of the Hudson River Valley stretches backward and forward in time. When the steamships left and the people with them and the stores were boarded up so many years ago, Tivoli seemed to have died. Now we know that, like Rip Van Winkle, the town was just taking a nap.

THE

Café Pongo

COOKBOOK

1

BREAKFAST

For its first two years of operation Café Pongo served only breakfast and lunch. We wanted our menu to complement the breads and baked goods we made in the bakery. After so many years of serving only dinner at Santa Fe, it was exciting to have a new palette of foods and flavors to choose from. Breakfast foods need not be limited to simple eggs, potatoes, and pancakes, as the following recipes reflect.

For people who enjoy the mornings and afternoons, a brunch party is an alternative to the dinner party. I find it more relaxing and simple to reciprocate a dinner party with a Sunday brunch. Guests usually arrive at around eleven. I'll make fresh juice and a pot of ginger lemon tea or mulled cider to get started. If alcohol is served, I choose a Vinho Verde, a crisp, slightly spritzy low-alcohol wine that is also very affordable. (Champagne or a bloody Mary usually means spending the remainder of the day napping.) At some point the group usually takes a hike outdoors or plays board games inside if there's bad weather. I end the meal, depending on the temperature, either with Thai iced coffee or homemade hot chocolate. By 5:00 P.M. dishes are washed and put away. A daytime brunch versus dinner party can be an inexpensive way to entertain as well as more conducive to outdoor activities. Whether cooking for guests or just someone special, don't underestimate the elegant and inviting possibilities of breakfast.

On the days when the task of making breakfast seems too arduous, remember that few things are quicker to prepare than eggs. The addition of fresh herbs, such as chervil, chives, or basil, to scrambled eggs makes the simple special. Add some smoked salmon and goat cheese and those six minutes spent in the kitchen will make you a cooking star. If the heat is driving you from the kitchen, do as they do in Mexico—serve fresh salsa with eggs. Salsa verde (page 37) is easy, but even easier is chopped fresh ripe tomatoes with a little onion, hot pepper, lime, and avocado slices. This complements eggs any style with crunch and flavor. Fresh herbs and ingredients are the key to cooking success and should not be forgotten at breakfast.

Poached Eggs

1 TO 3 EGGS PER PERSON

**2 tablespoons distilled white vinegar for
1 gallon water
1 to 3 eggs per person**

1. In a deep pan bring at least 3 inches water to a rolling boil. Pour in a generous splash of distilled white vinegar. The water should not have a strong vinegar smell. The vinegar in the water will help hold the eggs together so you don't make egg drop soup.
2. Gently crack the eggs into the water.
3. As soon as the whites look evenly cooked and no longer translucent, lift one egg out with a slotted spoon and check it for doneness. A poached egg should have a runny yolk. You can tell how runny the yolk is by gently poking its belly with your finger; if it jiggles like the Pillsbury Doughboy, it's done. If you like it firmer, gently resubmerge it. As it cooks the egg will become firmer and firmer until it's eventually hard-boiled. Poached eggs will stay warm for a minute or two set aside in a little dish.

Omelet Basies

Many cooks consider the omelet quite basic and simple, but I was once terrified of making omelets. When Pongo first went from being a bakery to a full-service restaurant, I had to train the brunch chefs. I had been cooking for over ten years at this point and had managed all kinds of cooking and catering but never short-order breakfast. The timing is so much faster, and people are very particular about how they like their eggs. Someone who likes eggs well done will not eat a runny omelet, and a soft-omelet eater will find an overcooked one inedible.

Most Americans seem to prefer their omelets cooked like pancakes—that is, fully done on both sides. In many American restaurants (including Pongo) omelets are placed under a broiler, which cooks the eggs all the way through as well as puffs them up, like a soufflé. The traditional French omelet is runny in the middle. It is cooked very quickly, never on both sides, and never browned.

My best advice is to use a good single-omelet-sized nonstick pan. Clarified butter will help to avoid browning. Stir from the bottom with a plastic spatula; do not overwork the eggs but pull the cooked outer edges toward the middle. Keep the pan moving over the heat. This method can get you almost all the way to well done. If you must have your eggs fully cooked on both sides and don't have a broiler, you can turn the omelet with a spatula or simply flip the omelet in the pan. Quickly flick your wrist (yes, the one holding the pan) upward with a small jerking motion toward yourself. Remember, eggs are cheap; just allow yourself enough time to scrub the stovetop. And the walls. When the omelet is fully cooked to your liking, add the fillings of your choice. A three-egg omelet will hold about ½ to ¾ cup filling. Squeeze in more if you do not mind the omelet not fully closed.

TASTY OMELET COMBINATIONS

1/2 TO 3/4 CUP OF ANY OF THE FOLLOWING PER 3-EGG OMELET

FANCY: Butter-braised onion, fresh sorrel, and goat cheese
Gruyère and prosciutto
Smoked salmon, chive, and goat cheese
Blanched asparagus and lemon-thyme ricotta
Sautéed portobello with Saga blue cheese and roasted red peppers (page 221)

FRIENDLY: Cream cheese and jelly
Feta, spinach, and black beans
Ratatouille and basil
Grilled tomato, caramelized onion (page 137), and Swiss cheese
Minced raw red onion, crisp minced bacon, and Swiss cheese

Whenever we have a new morning chef (morning chefs are often culinary students), many different sizes of stainless-steel bowls appear and multiple whisks are unsheathed. The atmosphere gets very serious.

Mikee and I just stand back and smile. We can make hollandaise in less than ten minutes. Ours has never broken. If we are busy, we bark out directions to anybody who happens to be around. Their hollandaise has never broken—and neither will yours—as long as you follow a few simple steps.

Hollandaise is so simple it's tricky. Remember, eggs can smell fear. If the hollandaise starts to separate, dump it out and start over. Once you've done this a couple of times, you'll become more brazen and start pouring in the hot butter faster. Keep the hollandaise at room temperature until ready to serve. When the sauce cools down, it gets very thick. The best way to slightly warm it and get the consistency back is to whisk in boiling water 2 tablespoons at a time.

2 large egg yolks	Juice of ¼ lemon (no seeds)
1 large egg	Salt and cracked pepper to taste
1 cup (2 sticks) butter	Dash of Durkee's red hot sauce

1. In a blender or with a standing mixer on medium speed, whip the egg yolks and egg until they start to get fluffy and turn from orange in color to a pale yellow.
2. Melt the butter in a small pan over low heat or in the microwave. Let it sit momentarily until the milk solids fall to the bottom. I microwave the butter in a small pitcher.
3. *Do not let the butter cool down!* Set the blender or mixer on the lowest speed. Pour the hot clarified butter *very slowly* into the eggs. If you pour too quickly, you will cook the yolks instead of emulsifying them.
4. When the eggs and butter are completely combined, add the lemon juice, salt, pepper, and hot sauce.

Breakfast Burritos

These are very quick and easy to make. The salsa can be made from scratch (see below) or purchased fresh. Most stores now carry good-quality fresh salsas—look for them in the refrigerated section.

2 tablespoons butter
6 to 8 eggs, lightly beaten
1/4 cup sliced roasted red peppers (page 221)
1/4 cup chopped scallions
1/4 cup crumbled feta cheese

1/4 cup grated Monterey Jack or Cheddar cheese
2 good-quality flour tortillas
Salsa Fresca (recipe follows)
Sour cream
Sliced pickled or fresh jalapeños

Melt the butter in a large nonstick skillet. Scramble the eggs with the peppers, scallions, and cheeses. Directly over a medium gas flame or in a heavy cast-iron skillet or comal, using tongs, warm the tortillas on both sides; they will rise with pockets of warm air. Immediately divide the eggs between the tortillas. Cut in half and serve with salsa, sour cream, and jalapeños.

SALSA FRESCA

YIELDS ABOUT 2 CUPS

2 ripe medium tomatoes, diced
1 medium red onion, diced
1 cucumber, peeled, seeded, and diced
2 cloves garlic, minced

1 serrano or 1/2 jalapeño pepper (more or less to taste), sliced
1/4 cup minced fresh cilantro
Juice of 3 limes
1 teaspoon sugar (optional)
Salt and cracked pepper to taste

Thoroughly mix all ingredients together; serve at room temperature.

Scrambled Egg and Chorizo Tacos with Plantains, Black Beans, and Avocado

This recipe makes a great dinner, too: replace the tacos with roast chicken and add salsa verde (page 37).

Fried plantains are one of my favorite foods. Plantains can be eaten ripe or when they are completely green. Most people seem to prefer their plantains riper and sweeter. I prefer them unripe and more savory.

PLANTAINS:

2 cups vegetable, peanut, or canola oil
3 to 4 plantains, ripe or unripe
1 tablespoon minced garlic
2 tablespoons Durkee's red hot sauce
1/2 cup water

TACOS:

2 tablespoons butter
8 to 12 eggs, lightly beaten
1 pound good-quality Spanish or Por-
   tuguese chorizo or Italian sopressata,
   minced
8 to 12 good-quality corn tortillas
2 to 3 cups grated mild Monterey Jack or
   Cheddar cheese
4 cups seasoned black beans (your favorite recipe or try Santa Fe Black
   Beans, page 216), heated through
2 perfectly ripe Haas avocados, peeled,
   pitted, and sliced
Crumbled feta cheese or queso fresco

FOR THE PLANTAINS:

1. In a deep cast-iron skillet over medium heat, begin to heat the oil.
2. Cut the ends off the plantains. Run a paring knife down the edges of the skin. Wedge the knife into the cut you have just made and turn the knife as if turning a key, prying off the skins. The riper the fruit the easier it is to peel. Cut the peeled plantains in 1-inch slices.
3. Mix the garlic, hot sauce, and the water. If the plantains are ripe, dip them in this liquid and, taking care to avoid spattering, fry them on both sides until they are golden brown, then dry them on a paper towel. If the plantains are unripe, fry the pieces until they are golden brown on both sides. Lay them on

a cutting board and smash them with the flat side of a knife. Dip them in the hot sauce mixture and fry them again until golden brown. Dry them on a paper towel.

FOR THE TACOS:

4. In a large skillet over medium heat, melt the butter. Add the eggs and chorizo and scramble.
5. On a griddle or in a large heavy skillet over medium heat, lay down the tortillas and sprinkle grated cheese on each one. Spoon on the scrambled eggs, fold the tortillas over, and reduce the heat to low. Cook until the cheese melts out and gets crispy and golden brown.
6. Scoop some black beans on one side of each person's plate. Arrange the plantains, tacos, and avocado slices on the plate and crumble the feta over the top.

Egg McMeg: Pesto Omelet Sandwich on Multigrain Bread with Caramelized Onions and Tomatoes

This simple and easy-to-make breakfast sandwich has become a staple at Café Pongo. Meg Aldrich, a one-time summer chef and friend of the Pongo family, made it one Saturday as a brunch special many years ago. Almost everyone who came in ordered it. For weeks after that, people kept asking for "that pesto sandwich." The Egg McMeg ended up on the menu and has remained there ever since.

> 4 slices Multigrain Walnut Bread
>   (page 263)
> 2 tablespoons butter
> 1 perfectly ripe tomato, cut in thick slices
> Caramelized Onions (page 137)
> Sliced or grated Cheddar cheese (optional)
> 6 eggs
> 3 tablespoons pesto, homemade (page 30)
>   or store bought

1. Have the bread in the toaster, ready to go.
2. Melt 1 tablespoon of the butter in a nonstick medium skillet over medium-high heat. Add the tomato with the caramelized onions and quickly brown the tomato slices on both sides. Reduce the heat. Lay the cheese over the tomato slices, cover the pan, and allow the cheese to melt.
3. Melt the remaining 1 tablespoon butter in a large nonstick skillet over medium heat. Whisk the eggs together and pour them into the butter. Using a plastic spatula, stir the eggs from the bottom. Stir in the pesto. Do not allow the eggs to turn brown. (Basically, you are making an omelet.)
4. Toast the bread.
5. Slide the tomato and onions into the center of the egg mixture. Fold the eggs around the onions and tomato. Gently shake the pan to make sure that the eggs are not stuck to the bottom. Cut the omelet in half.
6. Slide half the omelet onto one slice of toast. Top with another slice of toast and cut in half with a sharp serrated knife. If you don't think you can cut the sandwich without squashing it, cut the top piece of toast first, then lay it on top of the sandwich and follow the cut through the eggs and bottom piece of toast. Repeat with the second sandwich.

Traditional Eggs Benedict

Eggs Benedict is probably the most popular egg dish in the world. It consists of poached eggs set atop Canadian bacon on an English muffin with hollandaise sauce poured over. At Pongo our secret weapon is our homemade English muffins and really good-quality Canadian bacon or Italian pancetta. We also have many vegetarian variations. Most people reserve this treat for restaurants because it seems complicated to make at home. Okay, so hollandaise does take some getting used to; so does poaching eggs correctly. But it's just like learning to ride a bike—a little tricky at first but very simple once you get the hang of it. (Mikee, our baker, insists that English muffins are easy, too.) So some lazy Sunday give it try.

> 2 thick slices Canadian bacon per person (see Note)
> 2 eggs per person
> 1 very good-quality English muffin per person
> Hollandaise Sauce (page 22), at room temperature
> Cracked pepper to taste

1. Lay the bacon slices in a heavy skillet. Brown both sides over low heat until ready to serve.
2. Poach the eggs (page 20).
3. While the eggs are poaching, toast the English muffins. Using a broiler or a little butter in a large skillet or on a griddle works best. With a conventional toaster and four or more guests, the first toasted muffin will be cold before the last one gets in the toaster. The key to breakfast cooking (or any cooking, for that matter) is getting everything to come out hot at the same time.
4. Lay 2 toasted English muffin halves on each plate and place a slice of bacon on each half. Place a poached egg over the bacon and ladle the hollandaise over the top.
5. Season with cracked pepper and garnish with any combination of the following: flat-leaf parsley, sliced roasted red peppers (page 221), capers, watercress, fresh chervil, fresh basil, fresh purple basil, fresh dill, or thin lemon-wheel slices.

Note: Vegetarian alternatives to Canadian bacon include poached asparagus tips; roasted peppers; grilled or broiled portobello mushroom caps; wilted greens such as spinach, mustard, arugula, mizuna, lightly sautéed with garlic.

This variation of traditional eggs Benedict can be made with or without home-made smoked salmon. (Still, I encourage you to smoke your own!)

Hot smoking is much easier than cold smoking. The result is pink salmon that looks like it's poached but with a sweet, tangy, smoky flavor. Only a small hand-ful of mesquite chips are used so the salmon is not too smoky. The smoking can be done days ahead, and the fish can even be frozen afterward. This salmon can be used in pastas, crumbled into salads, made into an outstanding sandwich, used in steam pots (page 170), or added to any dish that calls for traditional smoked salmon.

You will need a covered container, at least three inches deep. (Aluminum foil can be used as a cover.) Inside the container there needs to be a rack or mesh grate that will hold the fish at least an inch above the wood chips. Air must be able to circulate around the container. A charcoal grill, devoid of all charcoal, can be used outdoors, but the heat is harder to control. A fish poacher will work as long as you don't mind the bottom getting a little sooty. I use a hotel pan (a deep oven pan) with a perforated insert, and cover the top with foil.

SALMON:

4 or more very fresh salmon fillets with skin, 8 to 10 ounces each
4 teaspoons maple syrup
Kosher salt
Mesquite wood chips (about ½ cup for 4 salmon fillets)
2 tablespoons good-quality organic Earl Grey tea leaves

SPINACH AND EGGS BENEDICT:

10 ounces fresh spinach, stems removed, washed and dried
2 tablespoons extra-virgin olive oil, plus more for the salmon
4 to 6 cloves garlic, minced
8 eggs
1 Baguette (page 260), cut in 4 equal pieces
Hollandaise Sauce (page 22), at room temperature
Cracked pepper to taste

FOR THE SMOKED SALMON:

1. Rinse and pat the salmon dry. Rub each fillet on both sides with about 1 teaspoon maple syrup and cover liberally with salt. Refrigerate the salted salmon for about 2 hours.

2. In the bottom of whatever you have rigged up for smoking, place the mesquite chips and tea leaves. Rinse all the salt off the salmon and lay the pieces *skin side down* on the grate in your "smoker." Cover tightly with a lid or with foil. Place this unit on the stove over medium to low heat. The cooking time will vary depending on the size of the vessel used and the amount of fish; generally 20 minutes is about right. I carry the whole assembly out to the back porch to check the salmon, as much of the smoke will escape when the smoker is opened. The salmon should be pink all the way through and flake off in sections. Salmon will also "bleed" white when it is cooked all the way. *Do not overcook the salmon!* Smoking, like many things, is very simple after one or two attempts. When the salmon is done, you can lift out the rack it is sitting on and leave the still-smoldering mesquite outside.

3. When the salmon has cooled, carefully remove it from the grate with a spatula; wrap each piece in plastic wrap and refrigerate or freeze it if you'll be using it later.

FOR THE SPINACH AND EGGS BENEDICT:

4. Quickly sauté the spinach with the 2 tablespoons oil and garlic in a large skillet over medium heat right before you are ready to serve.

5. Reheat the salmon with a dash of olive oil in a heavy skillet over medium heat until one side is golden brown and slightly crispy.

6. Poach the eggs (page 20) and set them aside; do not allow them to get too cool. Split each piece of baguette in half but don't cut all the way through. Toast the bread in the oven or under the broiler, then keep warm.

7. Divide the sautéed spinach among the toasts and balance the poached eggs on top. Lay the salmon over the eggs. Drizzle the salmon-flavored oil over the top. Cover with hollandaise sauce.

8. Season with cracked pepper and garnish with any combination of the following: flat-leaf parsley, roasted red peppers (page 221), capers, watercress, fresh chervil, fresh basil, fresh purple basil, fresh dill, or thin lemon-wheel slices.

This dish is a personal favorite of mine. The sharp fresh flavor of the parsley pesto combines well with the smoky, spicy-sweet flavor of the chipotle sauce. A fan of this dish once told me that it allows one to achieve the "perfect bite": the ultimate combination of soft and crisp, sweet and tangy, mild and spicy in one mouthful.

The pesto and chipotle sauce are both quick and easy. The chipotle sauce can be made hotter, but if it is made any milder, it would not be worth making, as chipotle peppers are the essential ingredient. If spicy food is not your thing, make a roasted red pepper coulis (page 32) instead; this will add beautiful color and a clean, fresh flavor. Both sauces are staples at Café Pongo. We use them for bread spreads, dips, with pasta, with shrimp, and in a host of other ways. They can also both be prepared days ahead of time.

If the sauces are made ahead of time, this recipe takes about as long as it does to boil water. Roasted potatoes with rosemary are a great accompaniment for this dish.

PESTO:

2 bunches flat-leaf parsley, washed and
   dried (reserve a few sprigs for garnish)
2 cups extra-virgin olive oil
1 cup almonds, blanched and sliced
4 cloves garlic
2 teaspoons grated lemon zest
1/4 cup fresh lemon juice
1 teaspoon salt
1/2 teaspoon pepper
1 cup grated Parmesan cheese
Chipotle Sauce (page 226)

TO FINISH THE DISH:

2 or 3 eggs per person
1/4 good-quality baguette per person
1 to 2 ounces soft and mild goat cheese
   per person
Roasted red pepper strips (page 221) for
   garnish

FOR THE PESTO:

1. Fill a food processor or blender with about two-thirds of the parsley. Add a little of the oil and purée. Slowly add the almonds, garlic, lemon zest, lemon juice, salt, and pepper. Slowly feed in the remaining parsley, the Parmesan, and the remaining oil.

FOR THE CHIPOTLE SAUCE:

2. Purée all the ingredients except the cilantro and tomato paste in a blender or food processor until evenly mixed.
3. Roughly chop the cilantro, add it to the blender, and quickly blend it in.
4. Pour the mixture into a bowl; then whisk in the tomato paste.

TO FINISH THE DISH:

5. Poach the eggs (page 20) and set them aside; do not allow them to cool.
6. Cut the pieces of baguette in half but not all the way through. Toast the bread. Spread the room-temperature pesto on the warm toast. Ladle the chipotle sauce on the bottom of each person's plate. Crumble the goat cheese over the chipotle sauce. Float the pesto-covered toast in the chipotle sauce and goat cheese. Slide the poached eggs onto the toast and garnish with parsley sprigs and roasted red pepper strips. Serve hot.

Variations on Pesto

For basil pesto, substitute basil for parsley and pine nuts or walnuts for almonds.

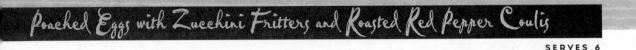

Poached Eggs with Zucchini Fritters and Roasted Red Pepper Coulis

SERVES 6

These are colorful, fresh tasting, and fairly healthy.

For a tasty variation, try the fritters by themselves with crumbled feta cheese and apricot jam on the side.

FRITTERS:

4 cloves garlic, minced
1 cup flat-leaf parsley, coarsely chopped (save a few whole sprigs for garnish)
1 tablespoon grated lemon zest
2 pounds zucchini, coarsely grated (6 cups)

1 cup all-purpose flour
4 large eggs, lightly beaten
2 cups vegetable, peanut, or canola oil
Salt and cracked pepper to taste

RED PEPPER COULIS:

3 cups Roasted Red Peppers (page 221)
1/4 cup olive oil

1/4 cup blanched almonds
Juice of 1 lemon (no seeds)
Salt and cracked pepper to taste

TO FINISH THE DISH:

8 eggs

FOR THE FRITTERS:

1. Fold together the garlic, parsley, and lemon zest. Stir in the grated zucchini, then the flour and eggs. Season with salt and cracked pepper.
2. Form the mixture into 20 thin 2-inch-wide cakes. Make sure the fritters are flat, not round like meatballs. This will ensure that they will cook all the way through. Heat the oil in a large skillet over medium-high heat. Add the fritters in batches and fry on both sides until golden brown.

FOR THE COULIS:

3. Combine all the ingredients in a blender or food processor until evenly puréed. Warm the coulis over low heat or in a microwave oven.

TO FINISH THE DISH:

4. The faster you can put this together the better, so that everything remains hot. The fritters are best right out of the skillet. Poach the eggs (page 20) and place 1 egg on top of 3 or 4 fritters for each serving. Spoon the warmed red pepper coulis over the eggs.

5. Garnish with freshly cracked pepper, flat-leaf parsley sprigs, and any of the following: roasted red pepper strips, watercress sprigs, shaved Romano or Parmesan cheese, fresh basil, fresh purple basil, or thin lemon wheels.

Frittata with Pancetta, Arugula, and Pasta

This can be served for breakfast or lunch or as tapas, hot or at room temperature. I love the taste of raw onion in eggs; if you agree, add more onion.

6 thick slices pancetta (Italian bacon)
3 cups cooked (al dente) capellini, broken
   in half before cooking
1 dozen eggs
1 tablespoon olive oil or butter
1/2 medium white onion, minced
2 cloves garlic, minced
1 bunch arugula, washed, dried, and
   chopped

1. In a large sauté pan over medium heat, fry the pancetta until it is crisp. Remove it from the pan. Do not discard the fat. Crumble the pancetta in small pieces and set aside.

2. In the fat of the pancetta over medium heat, brown the cooked capellini. Do not let the pasta stick. Reduce the heat.

3. Whisk the eggs together but do not overbeat them. Add the olive oil to the pan and pour the eggs over the pasta. Stir in the pancetta, onion, garlic, and arugula. Using a rubber spatula, stir from the bottom and keep loosening the eggs from the sides. When the eggs appear to be mostly cooked, shake the pan. The entire mass should move together in the pan. Loosen it anywhere it is sticking. Place a large plate over the pan and, holding the plate to the pan with one hand, flip the eggs onto the plate. Let this set for 5 minutes. Cut the frittata in triangular wedges.

SERVES 2

I have prepared this dish thousands of times. Many of our regulars insist that it has addictive qualities.

At Pongo, we use heatproof luncheon-size plates for the huevos rancheros. We then slide the luncheon plates onto larger dinner-size plates so the wait staff can pick them up without burning their hands. This dish can also be served family-style on as large a platter as your oven will hold. Allow one cup of beans and two to three eggs per person; add salsa and onions to taste (I love them, so I use a lot). I garnish with large sprigs of parsley. I enjoy the crunch of it with my beans. If you don't have flat-leaf parsley, roughly chop some curly parsley; cilantro is a nice addition as well. *¡Viva las frijoles!*

6 good-quality corn tortillas
2 cups Santa Fe Black Beans (page 216)
1 1/2 cups homemade or store-bought fresh
   salsa (not jarred)
1/4 cup Caramelized Onions (page 137)
4 ounces sharp Cheddar or Monterey Jack
   cheese, grated or sliced
4 to 6 eggs (depending on how hungry the
   two of you are), cooked any style
Flat-leaf parsley and/or cilantro sprigs
Avocado slices
Sour cream

1. Line 2 ovenproof plates with the corn tortillas.
2. Spread the beans over the tortillas, covering them to the edges to keep the tortillas from burning.
3. Spread ½ cup of the salsa and the onions over the beans. Cover everything with the cheese.
4. Broil until the cheese is a deep golden brown.
5. Top with the eggs and the parsley. Serve with the remaining salsa, the avocado, and sour cream on the side.

Scallion Cheddar Grits with Eggs Any Style, Salsa Verde, and Crispy Fried Onions

I have always felt a sense of mission in regard to grits. Grits are every bit as delicious as their popular counterpart the home-fried potato, but people from the Northeast and New England have rarely even tasted them. At Pongo, people get so excited when they try these scallion Cheddar grits they always pull me aside and ask a lot of questions like, "What are grits?" Well, grits are ground dried hominy. What is hominy? Hominy is the whole kernels of corn soaked in water and lime until the outer husk comes off, leaving swollen white corn kernels. Hominy can be purchased canned. It is wonderful sautéed in a little olive oil, lime juice, and dried chili.

Grits can be served two ways: soft like porridge or the way we serve them at Pongo. We pour the soft grits about an inch thick into a greased sheet pan and let them set. They are then cut into squares, brushed with a little butter, and broiled until they are crisp and golden brown on the outside and soft and creamy inside. The advantage to this method is that the cut grit squares can be prepared days ahead and kept cold.

For parties, I mix smoked Cheddar and shrimp into the grits and cut the cooled grits with a cookie cutter or the mouth of a white wineglass. These little grit cakes (page 131) can be made and kept chilled for up to a day. The cakes are then brushed with butter and either broiled or grilled or fried until they are crisp and browned, then served hot with cilantro crème fraîche.

I recommend serving the scallion Cheddar grits with salsa verde, eggs any style, and crispy fried onions. (Do not be intimidated by the tomatillos in salsa verde; they may look weird but they are quick and easy to prepare.) Salsa verde is very low in fat and full of flavor. It keeps well refrigerated so it can be made in advance. It is great eaten cold with chips or served hot with chicken, pork, tacos, enchiladas . . . the list goes on and on.

ONIONS:

2 cups vegetable, peanut, or canola oil
2 Spanish onions, sliced very thin
1 cup all-purpose flour

Salsa verde:

2 tablespoons olive oil
6 tightly packed cups coarsely chopped
fresh tomatillos (remove the husks and
rinse the fruit before chopping)
1 Spanish onion, minced
2 cloves garlic
1/4 cup chopped fresh cilantro leaves
1 teaspoon brown sugar

Grits:

3 quarts milk
8 tablespoons (1 stick) butter
1 cup chopped scallions
2 cups grated Cheddar cheese (smoked
Cheddar is really good if you can find
it)
Salt and cracked pepper to taste
4 cups quick grits
1 1/2 cups minced fully cooked shrimp or
bacon (optional)

To finish the dish:

2 or 3 eggs per person, cooked any style
Minced red bell pepper and cilantro sprigs
for garnish

For the onions:

1. Heat the oil in a deep fryer over medium heat to 375 degrees. Do not allow it to smoke.
2. Coat the onion slices with the flour and shake off the excess. Fry them in small batches in the oil until golden brown and dry them on paper towels. The onions should be crisp, like onion rings, not limp. If they seem a little limp, put them in a 250-degree oven until they crisp.

For the salsa verde:

3. Heat the oil in a deep heavy skillet over medium to low heat. Add the tomatillos, onion, and garlic and sauté until the tomatillos begin to soften.
4. In a blender or food processor, purée the tomatillo mixture. Stir in the cilantro and brown sugar.

For the grits:

5. In a deep, heavy soup pot, bring the milk to a slow boil. Add the butter, scallions, Cheddar, salt, and pepper. Slowly whisk in the grits and reduce the heat. Keep stirring from the bottom as the grits can stick. If the grits appear really dry, stir in water or more milk in the same way more broth is added to a risotto when it seems too sticky. The consistency you want is that of a thick porridge. Cook until the grits no longer taste too sandy or gritty. Stir in the shrimp or bacon, if using, and cook just until it is heated through. The grits can be served now.

   If you are making the grits ahead of time, grease a 12 × 17-inch pan and spread the still-hot grits in the pan. Use a rubber spatula dipped in melted butter to smooth the top of the grits. Let the grits cool to room temperature, then refrigerate them. When you are ready to serve, cut the grits into 6 to 8 equal-size pieces. Brush the tops with melted butter and broil until crisp and browned.

To finish the dish:

6. Heat the salsa verde until hot. Ladle about ¾ cup of the hot salsa verde over the bottom of each person's plate. Scoop the hot soft grits or place a hot, golden brown grit cake on the center of the salsa verde. Drape the eggs over the grits. Put a generous pile of fried onions on top and sprinkle the minced red pepper and cilantro sprigs around the edge of the plate. Serve with cracked pepper and extra salsa verde on the side.

Pongo's Special Scrambled Tofu Hash

We started making this for our customers who do not eat eggs or dairy. It is so good, however, that it does not need to be considered a substitute for anything. At Pongo we serve the tofu wrapped in a warm flour tortilla with roasted potatoes with rosemary, salsa verde (page 37), and chipotle sauce (page 226).

2 pounds extra firm tofu, cut into 1/2-inch cubes
2 cups peanut, olive, or canola oil
3/4 cup mushrooms marinated in 1/4 cup Café Pongo House Dressing (page 91), plus 2 tablespoons mushroom marinade
1/2 cup Caramelized Onions (page 137)
1/2 cup Roasted Red Peppers (page 221), sliced in strips
3/4 cup Santa Fe Black Beans (page 216) or any seasoned black beans
Salt and cracked pepper to taste

In a heavy skillet over medium heat, heat the oil. Add the tofu and brown it on both sides. Drain the tofu on paper towels, then pour off the oil in the pan. Return the tofu to the pan with all the remaining ingredients and simmer over low heat until warmed all the way through. Serve wrapped in warm tortillas or with toasted grain bread.

Red Flannel Salmon Hash

Beets give this dish its red color and a sweet flavor that works well with the salty, smoky taste of the salmon. Our homemade smoked salmon (page 28) is great for hash, but this dish can be made with any type of cooked or cured salmon. Fresh salmon fillets can be poached quickly in a little white wine with peppercorns and minced herbs, or you could use grilled salmon. Remember that hash is traditionally made from what is left over from dinner—fish, corned beef, roast beef, or chicken—so if you are preparing, say, grilled salmon, set aside two or three 8-ounce pieces for future use in this dish. The hash mixture can also be made a day or two ahead, making brunch preparation quick and easy.

At Pongo, we serve this hash with poached eggs (page 20) resting on top and with a horseradish hollandaise (add horseradish to taste to the hollandaise recipe on page 22).

1 cup peeled and minced potatoes
1 cup peeled and minced sweet
  potatoes (optional)
2 tablespoons butter or oil
1 onion, minced
1 cup minced celery
1 cup peeled and minced carrots
1 cup peeled and minced parsnips
  (see Note)

2 tablespoons fresh thyme leaves, or
  1 teaspoon dried thyme
1/4 cup dry vermouth or dry white wine
Three 6- to 8-ounce smoked or
  cooked salmon fillets (Pongo's
  smoked salmon on page 28 works
  great), skinned
1 1/2 cups cooked, peeled, and diced
  beets (see Note)

1. Boil the white potatoes, and sweet potatoes if using, until al dente. Drain well.
2. Heat the butter in a large sauté pan over medium heat. Add the onion, celery, carrots, parsnips, thyme, and vermouth and sauté until tender. Add the potatoes and a little more butter if the mixture is dry. Remove from the heat, crumble in the salmon, and stir in the beets.
3. When ready to serve, crisp a scoop of the hash in a small skillet with some butter or oil or pop the hash under a broiler with a little butter or oil on top.

Note: If parsnips are not available, prepare an extra cup of potatoes and/or sweet potatoes. Minced turnips can be used instead of or in addition to the parsnips as well.

Note: The beets can be omitted if you prefer a more traditional hash.

Roast Beef Hash

The beef can be roasted ahead of time or trimmed dinner leftovers can be used. This recipe is based on 1½ pounds beef. It can be stretched with less meat or "beefed up" with more. If there's no roast handy, you can cube some raw beef and pan-fry it with olive oil, salt, and pepper. Drain the fat and add the cooked beef to the veggies.

At Pongo we serve this hash with buttermilk scrambled eggs and chive biscuits (just add lots of freshly chopped chives to the biscuit dough on page 254).

> 1 cup peeled and minced potatoes
> 1 cup peeled and minced sweet potatoes
>   (optional)
> 2 tablespoons butter or oil
> 1 onion, minced
> 1 cup minced celery
> 1 cup peeled and minced carrots
> 1 cup peeled and minced parsnips
>   (see Note)
> 2 tablespoons fresh thyme leaves, or
>   1 teaspoon dried thyme
> 1½ pounds cooked choice beef, fat
>   trimmed, cut into ½-inch cubes
> 1½ cups dry red wine
> 1 tablespoon grated orange zest

1. Boil the white potatoes, and sweet potatoes, if using, until al dente. Drain well.

2. Heat the butter in a large sauté pan over medium heat. Add the onion, celery, carrots, parsnips, and thyme and sauté until tender. Add the potatoes and a little more butter if the mixture is dry. Remove from the heat. Add the roast beef, red wine, and orange zest. Return the skillet to the stove and let the beef simmer over low heat until the alcohol is cooked off and all the liquid is absorbed, 5 to 10 minutes. You may need to add a little water early on if it looks dry.

3. When ready to serve, crisp a scoop of the hash in a small skillet with some butter or oil or pop the hash under the broiler with a little butter or oil on top.

Note: If parsnips are not available, prepare an extra cup of minced potatoes. Minced turnips can be used instead of or in addition to the parsnips as well.

Hot pancakes, melting butter, and warm maple syrup are like a mother's hug on a cold morning. What better means of showing gastronomic love than making French toast? Dr. Atkins' grandmother must have been a lousy cook. How else could one forgo sweet corn cakes with sour cherries or poppy-seed almond pancakes. If you are a purist and insist on fruit-free pancakes, lay the bacon or sausage on top of a plain pancake and then pour on the maple syrup. (We all need a *little* protein!)

Pecan and Golden Raisin Oatmeal Brûlée

SERVES 4

This very cozy winter breakfast has been a staple on the Pongo brunch menu for many years. We serve the oatmeal with steamed golden raisins, pecans, and brown sugar crystallized on top. Using a blowtorch is the best way to melt the sugar—yes, a blowtorch. This is the same "kitchen tool" used for crème brûlée. At the café this oatmeal brûlée is lovingly referred to as the Papa Bear; to date, we have not yet come up with a Mama Bear.

This oatmeal is very good with homemade applesauce (page 225) served piping hot on the side. A dish of raspberries, blackberries, or strawberries is also a great side. Sometimes I slice ripe bananas over the oatmeal and then put the sugar mixture on top of them. The bananas taste really good with the sugar melted over them.

4 cups water
2 cups steel-cut oats (see Note)
1/2 cup pecan pieces
1/2 cup golden raisins
1 cup packed brown sugar
4 cups milk
1 vanilla bean, scraped, or 1 teaspoon
    pure vanilla extract
Maple syrup

1. Bring the water to a boil in a heavy saucepan and add the oats. Reduce the heat and simmer until the water is almost gone, about 20 minutes. Cover the pan tightly, remove it from the stove, and let sit until all the water is absorbed. Keep the oatmeal firm—do not let it get mushy. Remember it will continue to cook from its own heat when it is off the stove.
2. Scoop the oatmeal into an ovenproof serving dish. Mix the pecans, raisins, and brown sugar together and spread over the top of the oatmeal. Either melt this sugar mixture with a blowtorch or broil the dish until the mixture is golden brown, about 1 to 5 minutes.
3. If you have a cappuccino maker, steam the 4 cups milk with the vanilla. It looks beautiful when the milk has thick foam on top. If this is not an option, simply heat the milk with the vanilla on the stove. Serve the warm milk and maple syrup on the side.

Note: Steel-cut oats are oats that have not been rolled. I always thought that those little, flat ovals were oats in their natural state. I later learned that traditionally oats are first cut and then rolled flat. Steel-cut oats are those that haven't gone beyond that first step. The difference is a nuttier, chewier oat.

Pongo Granola

Store this winning mixture in a jar, and it will keep for a long time. Eat granola dry as a power snack or sprinkle it onto the wet side of pancakes before flipping them. Mush into ice cream. Top a fruit salad. Make a peanut butter, marmalade, and granola sandwich . . . the possibilities are endless. Why not double the recipe right now?

5 cups rolled oats (*not* quick oats)
1/2 cup sesame seeds
1/2 cup pecan pieces
1/2 cup walnut pieces
1/2 cup sliced almonds
1/2 cup (packed) brown sugar
6 1/2 tablespoons oil (corn, canola, saf-
   flower—any light, flavorless oil will do)
1/2 cup maple syrup
2 1/2 teaspoons pure vanilla extract

1. Preheat the oven to 400 degrees.
2. Toss together the dry ingredients, making sure to crush any errant lumps of brown sugar.
3. Mix the wet ingredients together; then pour over the dry mix and toss thoroughly.
4. Bake the granola on a baking sheet for 35 to 45 minutes, scraping and turning the mixture a few times to ensure even browning.

Phyllo Basket with Fresh Strawberries, Honey-Sweetened Ricotta, and Grand Marnier

This is a very light, fresh breakfast. Low-fat ricotta can be used for an even lighter dish. Use a good-quality honey, like a lavender honey, for example. This dish is very quick to prepare and dramatic in presentation. It can be served warm or cold. Everything can also be prepared ahead of time.

> 2 pints ripe strawberries in season
> 1/4 cup Grand Marnier liqueur
> 1/4 cup sugar
> 1 box (1 pound) phyllo pastry
> 1 pint ricotta cheese or good-quality
>   small-curd cottage cheese
> 1/4 teaspoon grated nutmeg
> 1/4 cup good-quality honey, or more to
>   taste
> Edible Johnny-jump-ups, mint sprigs, or
>   lavender blossoms for garnish

1. Preheat the oven to 400 degrees.
2. Slice the strawberries and combine them with the Grand Marnier and sugar. Let stand at room temperature.
3. Do not unfold the phyllo dough. Slice the rolled-up dough crosswise into 1-inch-thick strips.
4. On a baking sheet, gently unfold and loosen the strips of phyllo dough. (There is no need to grease the pan.) Lower the strips into 4 piles and very gently spread them out if they are piled too high. Be careful: if they are spread too thin they will fall apart. Bake the baskets until they are golden brown, 15 to 20 minutes. You should be able to carefully pick up the basket when it is done.
5. Combine ricotta, nutmeg, and honey.
6. Place a phyllo basket in the middle of each plate. Divide the ricotta into four scoops and place a scoop in the center of each basket. Ladle some strawberries and their juice in the center over the cheese. Garnish with Johnny-jump-ups (small, edible pansies), mint sprigs, or lavender blossoms. Dust the rim of the plate with nutmeg. Serve with a pot of honey on the side.

Plain and Simple Hotcakes

Nothing means Sunday quite like pancakes. There is noble purity in the plain, right-out-of-the-skillet pancake. But for those of you who cannot leave well enough alone, try adding some of the following: sliced banana, sliced apple, fresh blueberries, strawberries, sliced juicy peach, sliced kiwis, pitted ripe cherries, granola (page 44), toasted coconut, chocolate chips. I do not support the mixing of fruit into the batter, however; keep the batter plain, have the fruit all cut up, quickly lay your extras onto the wet side of the pancakes just before flipping them. This way you can make cool patterns. Serve pretty side up. Impress your guests; impress yourself.

> 2 cups sifted all-purpose flour
> 6 tablespoons sugar
> 2½ teaspoons baking powder
> 1 teaspoon salt
> 3 large eggs, slightly beaten
> 6 tablespoons melted butter
> 2 to 2½ cups milk
> Additional butter for cooking the
> pancakes (see Note)

1. Sift together the dry ingredients.
2. With a hand mixer or whisk, combine the wet ingredients. Mix the liquid ingredients quickly into the dry ingredients. Do not overmix.
3. Heat a griddle over medium heat. Add about 1 tablespoon butter to the griddle and heat until it is bubbling. If the butter smokes, reduce the heat. With a ¼-cup ladle, drop batter for each pancake onto the griddle. Cook until bubbles appear, then turn and cook the second side. If you are adding fruit, make sure the batter is cooked all the way through, particularly around the fruit. The fruit burns easily, so you may have to flip the pancake back and forth until it is done.

Note: I personally believe that pancakes should be cooked only in butter (or bacon fat, but I can't admit that publicly).

Plain and Simple Crêpes

Among my earliest restaurant memories is eating at the Magic Pan in my home-town of Philadelphia. I remember the crêpes were made in the dining room on a gigantic wheel of heated pans. The crêpe chef would stand in the center of the wheel and dip the bottom of the pans in batter, then flip them off when they had gone around the wheel once. They took exactly one time around to cook to per-fection, and the crowd was dazzled—myself included. I begged for a crêpe maker for Christmas.

By the eighties, the Magic Pan became a sushi bar. I, however, never lost my loyalty to crêpes. They are simple to make and can be enjoyed sweet for break-fast or savory for dinner. The batter is better if it stands overnight, but this is not imperative.

1 cup all-purpose flour
1 tablespoon sugar
2 large eggs or 3 medium ones
1¼ cups milk
1 teaspoon pure vanilla extract
¼ cup ginger ale, Sprite, or seltzer
Butter for cooking the crêpes

1. Mix all the ingredients except the ginger ale together until the batter is smooth and free of lumps, then stir in the ginger ale. Let the batter stand overnight.

2. Wipe a little butter, as though greasing a cookie sheet, over the bottom of an 11½-inch skillet over medium to low heat. Pour in just enough batter to cover the bottom of the pan in a thin layer. Cook the crêpe until the underside is golden brown. Loosen the crêpe, flip it over, and cook it lightly on the other side. The first crêpe, like your first pancake, is usually a flop, so don't get dis-couraged.

3. Fill with your favorite fruits, nuts, and berries, then roll up and eat. Some possibilities:

Nutella spread on the inside with sliced ripe bananas
    sautéed in butter
Sliced fresh strawberries on the inside and whipped
    cream with bittersweet chocolate shavings on top
Sliced honeydew melon on the inside and prosciutto
    "roses" on top
Sliced poached pear on the inside and pomegranate
    seeds sprinkled on top

Sour Cherry Corn Cakes

These crisp, sweet corn cakes are a unique twist on the traditional pancake. Using Jiffy corn muffin mix (the little blue boxes) makes this about as simple as it gets. Don't substitute other brands for they often use a finer grade of cornmeal, eliminating that gritty bite that makes the corn cakes so good. If fresh cherries are not available, use canned or jarred sour cherries in their own juice. They are in the canned fruit section, not the baking section, of the supermarket. *Do not use cherry pie filling.*

> 2 cups fresh or canned pitted sour
>   cherries, drained
> 1/4 cup sugar
> 2 tablespoon Chambord liqueur
> 1/2 teaspoon grated lemon zest
> 1 box Jiffy corn muffin mix
> 1 large egg
> 3/4 cup milk
> 2 tablespoons melted butter, plus
>   additional butter for cooking the
>   cakes

1. Combine the cherries, sugar, Chambord, and lemon zest. Let sit for about an hour or longer.
2. Combine the muffin mix, egg, milk, and melted butter. The batter will be thick.
3. In a cast-iron skillet or griddle over medium heat, heat about 1 tablespoon butter until the butter is bubbling. Drop about ¼ cup of the batter into the skillet for each corn cake. Spoon the cherries onto the wet side of the corn cakes. The corn batter is a little thicker than pancake batter and will not bubble through as much when it is ready to be flipped. Lift up an edge and peek underneath; when it is golden brown, flip it over. Make sure the batter is cooked all the way through, particularly around the cherries. The fruit will burn easily, so you may have to flip the cakes back and forth until they are done.

Brandied Apple Pancakes with Maple Crème Fraîche

This dish is quick, easy to make, and looks splashy for company. As with any dish that requires fresh fruits and vegetables, quality is of utmost importance. Fall in the Hudson Valley will make you rethink your idea of what a good apple is: Gala, Honey Crisp, Swiss Gourmet, Cameo, Golden Russet, Cox's Orange Pippin (Mikee's favorite), and Jonagold are newly emerging varieties of apples. At Pongo we are lucky to have them grown nearby at the orchard of the historic Hudson River estate Montgomery Place. Jonagold is the most popular apple in Europe; it is becoming increasingly available here in the states, as are Honey Crisps and Golden Russets. Look for them; *ask* for them.

Bisquick makes an excellent pancake, but if you prefer to make batter from scratch, make the Plain and Simple Hotcakes (page 47).

APPLES:
- ½ cup golden raisins
- ½ cup Cognac
- 10 firm tart apples
- 4 tablespoons (½ stick) butter
- ½ cup pecan pieces

PANCAKES:
- 2 cups Bisquick baking mix
- 1 to 2 large eggs
- 1 to 2 cups milk, depending on how thin you like your pancakes

CRÈME FRAÎCHE:
- 1 pint sour cream
- ½ cup maple syrup
- ¼ teaspoon grated nutmeg

TO FINISH THE DISH:
- Butter for cooking the pancakes
- Whole cinnamon sticks, crushed with the flat side of a knife

FOR THE APPLES:

1. Cover the raisins with boiling water and let soak until they are bloated and soft. Pour off the water and cover them with the Cognac.
2. Cut the "cheeks" off of the apples, bypassing their cores. Lay the apple "cheeks" on their flat sides and thinly slice. Cut the remaining fruit from the sides of the core, lay those pieces skin side up, and slice them. You will have perfect uniform slices with this method. Set aside a third of the slices to add to the pancakes while they're cooking.
3. In a heavy sauté pan over medium heat, melt 2 tablespoons of the butter.

Add the pecans and swirl them around until they start to brown. Scoop them out and set aside. Add two-thirds of the sliced apples and the remaining butter and increase the heat. Brown the apples quickly before they become applesauce. Add the brandied raisins and ignite the concoction. This is easiest to do by tilting the pan slightly so that the alcohol catches the gas flame, but you can also use a match. When the flame dies, the alcohol has cooked off. Add the toasted pecans and remove from the heat. You may have to reheat this sauce when you are ready to put it on the pancakes.

FOR THE PANCAKES:

4. Follow the Bisquick recipe (Bisquick is designed to make an all-American lumberjack's pancake—very bready—and perfect if you're the type who likes to think about cutting wood but ends up sawing logs about 20 minutes after eating them. I prefer a thin, crisp pancake, so I add twice the milk. This is a personal choice, so thin the batter with milk to your desired thickness.) Do not overstir the batter; you should be able to see a few small lumps. Try to fold the batter instead of whipping it.

FOR THE CRÈME FRAÎCHE:

5. Traditional crème fraîche is equal parts heavy cream and sour cream mixed and left to stand at room temperature overnight. But who has time for that? And think about the bacteria! So here's a quick and simple way to cheat: Mix the sour cream, maple syrup, and nutmeg until smooth. How's that for simplicity? Serve at room temperature.

TO FINISH THE DISH:

6. In a cast-iron skillet or on a griddle over medium heat, melt 1 tablespoon butter until it is bubbling. Drop ¼ cup of the batter for each pancake into the skillet. Cook until you can see bubbles coming up through the batter. Arrange the uncooked apple slices in a star or pinwheel pattern on each pancake. Flip the pancakes and cook the other side. Make sure that the batter is fully cooked, particularly around the apple slices. The fruit burns easily, so you may have to flip the pancake back and forth until it is done.

7. Arrange 3 pancakes apple side up on each person's plate. Put a large spoonful of crème fraîche in the center of each plate, and top with the hot sautéed apples. "Haystack" some of the crushed cinnamon sticks on top of each plate. Serve immediately.

SERVES 4

This is a seasonal variation of the brandied apple pancakes on page 50. The brandied apple pancakes are perfect for the fall, while the cranberry-clementine variation is a perfect winter holiday breakfast. It is best if the crème fraîche and the cranberry mixture can sit overnight.

Fresh clementines help me survive winter. They are not usually sold loose but come packed in little wooden crates. You only need six clementines for this recipe, but the remainder will get eaten quickly. (Save the delicate wooden crates and line them with tissue as gift boxes for assorted small gifts.) To me clementines taste distinctly like Christmas.

CRANBERRIES:

6 clementines, zest grated (see Note)
   and fruit juiced
1 cup sugar
1/2 bag fresh cranberries

CRÈME FRAÎCHE:

1 pint sour cream
1/2 cup maple syrup
1/4 teaspoon grated nutmeg

PANCAKES:

2 cups Bisquick baking mix
1 to 2 eggs
1 to 2 cups milk, depending on how thin
   you like your pancakes
Butter for cooking the pancakes

FOR THE CRANBERRIES:

1. Combine the juice of the clementines with *half* of the clementine zest, the sugar, and cranberries. Let stand overnight. Drain them before using.

FOR THE CRÈME FRAÎCHE:

2. Combine the sour cream, maple syrup, nutmeg, and the remaining clementine zest. Let stand overnight. Serve at room temperature.

FOR THE PANCAKES:

3. Follow the Bisquick recipe, thinning the batter with milk to your desired thickness. Do not overstir the pancake batter; try to fold the batter instead of whipping it.

4. In a cast-iron skillet or on a griddle over medium heat melt 1 tablespoon butter until it is bubbling. Drop ¼ cup of the batter for each pancake into the skillet. Cook until you can see bubbles coming up through the batter. Sprinkle some of the cranberries over the pancakes. Flip the pancakes and cook the other side. Make sure that the batter is fully cooked, particularly around the cranberries. The fruit burns easily, so you may have to flip the pancake back and forth until it is done.

5. Arrange 3 pancakes cranberry side up in a clover pattern on each person's plate. Put a large spoonful of clementine crème fraîche in the center of each plate. Garnish with more of the drained cranberries. Serve immediately.

Note: Forget using a box grater to zest citrus. All the zest gets caught between the holes and a lot of the bitter white pith gets mixed in. I much prefer the new flat, long Microplane zester. With this tool, the zest comes out finer, does not need to be chopped up, and miraculously takes only the zest with no pith. You will surely wonder how you survived without this wonder tool.

Toasted Coconut Pancakes with Caramelized Pineapple and Ginger Compote

These pancakes are exotic, delicious, stylish, and ridiculously easy to make.

PINEAPPLE COMPOTE:

> 2 ripe or overripe pineapples
> 1/2 cup packed brown sugar
> 1/2 cup golden raisins
> 1 tablespoon minced fresh ginger
> Captain Morgan's spiced rum (optional)
> 2 cups sweetened coconut flakes

PANCAKES:

> 2 cups Bisquick baking mix
> 1 to 2 eggs
> 1 to 2 cups milk (depending on how thin
> you like your pancake batter)
> Butter for cooking the pancakes

FOR THE PINEAPPLE COMPOTE:

1. Cut the tops and bottoms off the pineapples. Sit each pineapple on its flat end and cut the rinds off the sides. Cut the pineapples crosswise into ¼-inch-thick slices.

2. In a heavy skillet or on a griddle over medium heat, slowly brown (caramelize) both sides of the pineapple slices. Chop the browned pineapple. If the pineapple is ripe, you can chop the core as well. If the core is hard, cut it out. Try to reserve all the juice.

3. In a saucepan, simmer the chopped pineapple with its juices and the brown sugar, raisins, ginger, and rum, if using. Keep warm over low heat until you are ready to serve.

4. In a 400-degree oven, toast the shredded coconut on an ungreased sheet pan. (This goes very quickly. If need be you can toast it in small batches in the toaster oven.) Keep stirring the coconut until it browns evenly. Toasted coconut is so good you may want to keep it around for other uses. At the café, we use it as a garnish for our green curry shrimp and veggie fritters.

FOR THE PANCAKES:

5. Follow the Bisquick recipe, thinning the batter with milk to your desired thickness. Do not overstir the pancake batter; try to fold the batter instead of whipping it.

6. In a cast-iron skillet or on a griddle over medium heat, melt 1 tablespoon butter until it is bubbling. Drop ¼ cup of the batter for each pancake into the skillet. Cook until you can see bubbles coming up through the batter. Sprinkle some of the toasted coconut onto each pancake. Flip the pancakes over and cook the other side until the batter is fully cooked.

7. Arrange the pancakes coconut side up on serving plates. Ladle the hot pineapple compote over the pancakes. Garnish with more coconut.

Note: When a fruit or vegetable is slowly sautéed, it releases its natural sugars and turns brown, which is what caramelize means—to create caramel by browning the sugar.

This is my personal favorite of all the pancake/hotcake variations. I love the flavor of poppy seeds. I like poppy seed cake best when it is almost bluish black with seeds. The addition of almonds and maple cream to this recipe sends it past the moon.

MAPLE CREAM:

4 tablespoons (1/2) stick butter
1/2 cup maple syrup
1 cup heavy cream
1 teaspoon pure vanilla extract
1 teaspoon cornstarch dissolved in
   1 tablespoon water

ALMONDS:

1 cup slivered almonds
1 tablespoon butter

HOTCAKES:

1/4 cup almond paste
2 to 3 cups milk, depending on how thin
   you like your pancakes
1/4 cup amaretto liqueur
2 tablespoons pure almond extract
1/2 cup poppy seeds
4 cups Bisquick baking mix
3 large eggs
Butter for cooking the hotcakes
Powdered sugar for garnish

FOR THE MAPLE CREAM:

1. In a heavy saucepan over low heat, melt the butter with the maple syrup. Whisk in the cream, vanilla, and cornstarch mixture. Simmer over very low heat until ready to serve.

FOR THE ALMONDS:

2. In a sauté pan over medium heat, toast the almonds in the butter until golden brown.

FOR THE HOTCAKES:

3. In a food processor or blender, liquefy the almond paste with 2 cups of the

milk. Follow the Bisquick recipe using this almond milk. Gently stir in the amaretto, almond extract, and poppy seeds. Thin the batter with the remaining milk to your desired thickness. Do not overstir the pancake batter; you should be able to see a few small lumps. Try to fold the batter instead of whipping it.

4. In a cast iron skillet or on a griddle over medium heat, melt 1 tablespoon butter until it is bubbling. Drop ¼ cup of the batter for each pancake into the skillet. Cook until you can see bubbles coming up through the batter. Flip the pancakes over and cook the other side.

5. Arrange the pancakes on individual plates. Ladle a little hot maple cream over them and sprinkle a stripe of toasted almonds over top. Dust with powdered sugar. Serve immediately.

SERVES 4

This recipe was given to us by Lula's grandmother Sally. Light and fluffy on the inside and crisp on the outside, these have been a family favorite for many years. You can make the pancakes by themselves and eat them with whipped cream and/or maple syrup, but they are best with the blueberry compote Lula's dad (Roland) created. If the opportunity arises to make this recipe with Meyer lemons, jump on it. The recipe is very good with standard lemons, but with Meyer lemons it is pure heaven.

COMPOTE:

½ cup sugar
4 cups fresh or frozen whole blueberries
2 tablespoons Pernod or Sambuca liqueur
½ teaspoon fresh lemon juice
1 teaspoon cornstarch if needed

FLAPJACKS:

1 cup cottage cheese
1 tablespoon brown sugar
3 tablespoons fresh lemon juice
2 teaspoons grated lemon zest, plus
   additional for garnish
3 large eggs, separated
1 teaspoon pure vanilla extract
2 tablespoons olive or vegetable oil
2 teaspoons baking powder
½ cup all-purpose flour
¼ teaspoon salt
Butter for cooking the flapjacks
Powdered sugar for garnish

FOR THE COMPOTE:

1. Combine all the ingredients except the cornstarch in a saucepan and simmer over very low heat. As the berries heat up they will release their water. Frozen berries release a lot more liquid, so you may want to add a little cornstarch if the compote is too thin. If in the beginning it seems the berries are sticking to the bottom of the pan, add a splash of water, not too much.

FOR THE FLAPJACKS:

2. In a food processor, combine the cottage cheese, brown sugar, lemon juice, lemon zest, egg yolks, vanilla, and olive oil. Slowly add the baking powder, flour, and salt while the machine is running. Scrape the mixture into a bowl.

3. With an electric mixer, whip the egg whites until stiff peaks begin to appear. Gingerly fold the egg whites into the batter until all the ingredients are combined.

4. In a cast-iron skillet or on a griddle over medium heat, melt 1 tablespoon butter until it is bubbling. Drop ¼ cup of the batter for each flapjack into the skillet. Cook until you can see bubbles coming up through the batter. Flip the flapjacks over and cook the other side.

5. Place the flapjacks on individual plates and spoon the hot compote over the flapjacks. I make a stripe with the compote so that I can still see the lemon cakes underneath. Garnish with lemon zest and powdered sugar.

French Toast with Meyer Lemon Curd

When I was young and foolish, I assumed that recipes calling for Meyer lemons were simply pretentious. What did I know? I was living in Philadelphia, and I'd never been West, where Meyer lemons are more common. Then I tried one. There was no comparison to a standard lemon. I wouldn't waste squeezing a Meyer lemon over fried fish—the acidity of standard lemons is necessary in that instance. But for baking the floral scent of the Meyer lemon shines through. Because the Meyer is about four times sweeter than an ordinary lemon, the peels are far less bitter and more flavorful and, therefore, should not be wasted. The peels can be candied, put in marinades or pickling brine, or shaved over salads.

Meyer lemons are available November through March. They are thin skinned and do not ship easily, which makes them pricey, but they are well worth it. Do not miss them. This recipe is very simple, allowing all the subtleties of the Meyer lemon to be appreciated.

LEMON CURD:

10 or 11 Meyer lemons
4 cups sugar
8 large eggs, lightly beaten
2 tablespoons butter

FRENCH TOAST:

2 cups milk or cream
6 large eggs, lightly beaten
1/2 teaspoon ground allspice
1 teaspoon pure vanilla extract
2 good-quality day-old baguettes, thinly
   sliced on a diagonal, left to dry
   overnight or lightly toasted
Butter for cooking the French toast
Powdered sugar, thin lemon wheels, and
   Johnny-jump-ups (small, edible
   pansies) for garnish

FOR THE LEMON CURD:

1. Grate ½ cup zest from the lemons and squeeze 1 cup lemon juice. Set aside any remaining lemons for the garnish.

2. In a heavy saucepan over low heat, whisk the lemon juice and sugar until the sugar is dissolved. Add the lemon zest. Reduce the heat to as low as it will go and very slowly whisk in the beaten eggs. Drop in the butter and stir un-

til it is melted. Pour the mixture through a sieve or strainer. There will be a thick mixture of zest and cooked egg left in the strainer; set this aside. Return the strained lemon curd to the original pan. Gently reheat the curd over very low heat just before serving it.

FOR THE FRENCH TOAST:

3. Whisk together the milk, eggs, allspice, and vanilla. Dip the dry bread slices one or two at a time into this mixture. On a griddle or in a heavy skillet over low heat, melt 1 to 2 tablespoons butter until it is bubbling. Add as many slices of the bread as will fit and brown on both sides.
4. On individual plates, stack the hot French toasts 3 or 4 high, spreading the thick curd that was left in the sieve between the layers. Pour the warm lemon curd over the top. Garnish with powdered sugar, lemon wheels, and johnny-jump-ups.

2

SOUPS

Soup can be both extremely healthy and efficient. There is no better way to use kitchen scraps like onion and garlic skins, carrot tops and celery stumps, not to mention forgotten treasures like shrimp shells and, most prized of all, lobster shells. If the time to make stock is not available, don't give up. Like most things in life, great stocks can be bought. Once made, stock is easily portioned into smaller containers and frozen. With a little bit of planning, a healthy meal can be waiting at home for probably under a dollar per serving. (Even the chunkiest of canned soups, no matter what untensil one uses to eat it, does not compare with *real* soup.)

Stock—chicken, vegetable, or fish—instead of water improves the taste of almost any recipe, so it is a very good idea to always have some around. The amount and types of ingredients in your stockpot will always vary. The hardest part of making stock is having all the stuff you need; the trick is to make the stock when the ingredients are around and freeze it until you need it. You can make a vegetable stock on a day when you're making something with a lot of vegetables. Chicken bones, meat bones, or shrimp shells can be frozen to await the fresh vegetables.

Nothing is more cozy than the smell of a simmering stockpot, which can improve one's mood far better than any antidepressant on the market.

Okay, that's great for those who've got the time, but the latest statistics show that Americans are now on average working longer hours than even the Japanese. So when are we going to have the time to make both the soup and the stock (no matter how much euphoria the simmering stock might impart)? Fear not. There are many good canned stocks available, as well as the good ol' bouillon cube. The biggest problem with these is that they tend to be quite salty. I recommend using unsalted varieties of your favorite packaged stocks, then adding the salt yourself. This way you have better control of the end results.

Basic Vegetable Stock

The exact amounts of ingredients and the quantity of stock will vary.

> 1 to 2 tablespoons olive oil or more if
>   you're using a lot of vegetables
> Quartered onions with skins intact
> Celery stalks and leaves
> Carrots (see Note)
> Parsnips (see Note)
> Fennel stalks and tops
> Whole garlic bulbs, cut in half, with skins
>   intact
> Mushroom stems (particularly portobello
>   stems, which add a rich, beefy flavor)
> Fresh parsley stems with or without leaves
> Thyme sprigs, rosemary stems, or other
>   appropriate fresh herb sprigs or stems
>   (but not mint)
> 1 to 2 tablespoons whole peppercorns

1. The trick to getting the most flavor out of your ingredients is to roast them before you boil them. In a 350-degree oven, roast the larger vegetables with a little olive oil drizzled over them until they begin to brown. (Do not roast the parsley or herbs.)

2. Scrape the roasted vegetables with all the drippings into a stockpot, then add the other ingredients. Cover the vegetables with water (use spring water if you have bad-tasting water). Let the stock simmer over very low heat for several hours. Taste the stock; when it tastes rich and flavorful it is done. Pour it through a sieve or strainer. Be sure to press all the liquid from the vegetables before discarding them. If the stock tastes watery after it has simmered, there were probably not enough vegetables. You can always add a couple of bouillon cubes.

Note: Peel the carrots and parsnips if they are not organic; sometimes the peel can add a bitter flavor. The green carrot tops, however, are completely welcome.

You can get fresh fish heads, tails, and bones at any fish market. You might even get them for free. Salmon is easy to find and very good for stock. Shrimp, lobster, or crab shells also make outstanding stock.

Quartered onions with skins intact
Celery stalks and leaves
Carrots (see Note)
Parsnips (see Note)
Fennel stalks and tops
Whole garlic bulbs, cut in half, with skins
    intact
Very fresh fish heads (gills removed),
    tails, and bones, and/or shrimp,
    lobster, or crab shells
Thyme sprigs, rosemary stems, or other
    appropriate fresh herb sprigs or stems
    (but not mint)
1 to 2 tablespoons whole peppercorns

1. Roast the vegetables if you like as directed for Vegetable Stock (page 65).
2. Place all the ingredients in a stockpot and cover with water (use spring water if you have bad-tasting water). Simmer over low heat for several hours. Add more water if needed to keep the ingredients covered. Taste the stock; when it tastes rich and flavorful it is done. Pour the stock through a sieve or strainer. Be sure to press all the liquid from the solids before discarding them. If the stock tastes watery after it has simmered, you can always add a couple bottles of clam juice and/or some vegetable bouillon cubes.

Note: Peel the carrots and parsnips if they are not organic; sometimes the peel can add a bitter flavor. The green carrot tops, however, are completely welcome.

Basic Chicken or Meat Stock

Bones and scraps from 1 or more chickens
(necks and gizzards are very good,
too), or beef, pork, or pig's feet
(see Note)
1 to 2 tablespoons olive oil
Quartered onions, with skins intact
Celery stalks and leaves
Carrots (see Note)
Parsnips (see Note)
Fennel stalks and tops
Whole garlic bulbs, cut in half, with skins
intact
Fresh parsley stems, with or without
leaves
Thyme sprigs, rosemary stems, or other
appropriate fresh herb sprigs or stems
(but not mint)
1 to 2 tablespoons whole peppercorns

1. The trick to getting the most flavor out of your ingredients is to roast them before you boil them. In a 400-degree oven, roast all the chicken parts or meat bones, lightly coated with oil, in a roasting pan until browned. The larger vegetable scraps can be oiled and roasted, too, in a separate pan; they will brown faster than the meat. Do not roast the parsley or herbs.

2. Scrape everything from the roasting pans into a stockpot.

3. Add the remaining ingredients and cover with water (use spring water if you have bad-tasting water). Simmer over low heat for several hours. Add more water if needed to keep the ingredients covered. Taste the stock; when it tastes rich and flavorful it is done. Pour the stock through a sieve or strainer. Be sure to press all the liquid from the solids before discarding them. If the stock still tastes watery after it has simmered, there were probably not enough vegetables or bones. You can always add a couple of bouillon cubes to enhance the flavor. Immediately discard the small foil wrappers and no one will have to know.

Note: Pig's feet may seem barbaric, but if you eat pork, it is respectful to the animal to use all its parts. The Eskimos taught us this. Also, feet (pig and chicken) make a rich, deep-flavored stock.

Note: Peel the carrots and parsnips if they are not organic; sometimes the peel can add a bitter flavor. The green carrot tops, however, are completely welcome.

SERVES 8

Sugar snap peas are probably best eaten raw, to enjoy their pure, clean flavor. This soup muddies the flavor as little as possible. The peas are blanched momentarily in the stock, which leaves the soup, after it has been puréed, a bit crunchy, like a gazpacho. The pale green color makes it the quintessential spring soup. It is not heavy, so it is the perfect start to a big meal, such as an Easter dinner.

For this soup, the vegetable stock should *not* contain mushrooms, as they impart too much flavor and you'll lose the subtle sweetness of the peas.

1 large Vidalia onion, minced
1 tablespoon butter
2 tablespoons olive oil
4 cups chicken or vegetable stock
   (page 67 or 65)
1 pound sugar snap peas, ends trimmed
1/2 cup heavy cream
2 tablespoons minced fresh mint leaves,
   plus small sprigs for garnish
Salt and cracked pepper to taste
Crème fraîche, clotted cream, or sour
   cream for serving
Minced radishes for garnish (see Note)

1. In a heavy stockpot over medium heat, sauté the onion in the butter and oil until translucent. Add the stock and bring to a rolling boil. Drop in the sugar snap peas and let boil for 1 minute. Remove from the heat and let cool slightly.
2. Purée the soup and stir in the cream, mint, and salt and pepper. Allow the soup to cool to room temperature, then chill in the refrigerator.
3. Serve with a dollop of crème fraîche in the center of the bowl. Garnish with minced radish and mint sprigs.

Note: For a colorful garnish, slice the sides off the radish, discard the center, and mince the red sides.

White Gazpacho

This soup is ready in the time it takes to chop the vegetables. It is cool and soothing on hot summer days. This can also be used as a sauce over meaty white fish, such as halibut poached in white wine and garlic. Use a slotted spoon to ladle it over the fish.

4 large cucumbers, peeled, cut lengthwise in half, seeded, and diced (see Note)
3 celery stalks, leaves removed, cut into 1/4-inch cubes
1 small red onion, minced
1/2 green bell pepper, cut into 1/4-inch cubes
1 cup coconut milk
Juice of 1 lime
2 tablespoons minced fresh cilantro leaves
1 tablespoon minced fresh basil leaves, preferably purple basil
1/2 teaspoon garam masala
Salt and cracked pepper to taste

Combine all the ingredients together and chill in the refrigerator.

Note: If you are using unwaxed Kirby or unwaxed organic cucumbers, the skins may be left on; otherwise they should be peeled.

SERVES 8

This soup is perfect for that not-so-perfect bumper crop of tomatoes you may have around in late summer. If you are not a gardener, many farmstands sell slightly bruised tomatoes for less than half price. Sometimes chervil is hard to find, but please try; even if you have to grow it yourself, it's worth the effort. The flavor of chervil is somewhere between anise and cilantro with some utterly unique flavors mixed in.

> 2 whole garlic bulbs
> Extra-virgin olive oil
> 8 to 10 overripe or slightly bruised toma-
> toes
> Salt and cracked pepper to taste
> 4 cups vegetable or chicken stock
> (page 65 or 67)
> Fresh chervil leaves, coarsely chopped

1. Here's the bad news: preheat the oven to 475 degrees. The good news is the oven will not have to stay on long.
2. Cut the tops off the whole garlic bulbs and rub off just the loose outer skins. Pour olive oil into the open tops and roast in a pie pan in the oven until soft and deep golden brown, about 20 minutes.
3. On a baking sheet, place the whole tomatoes stem side down. Drizzle with olive oil and sprinkle with salt and pepper. Roast until they are well browned on top.
4. Let the roasted vegetables cool until you can handle them without pain. With your hands, gently remove the stems and seeds from tomatoes (you don't have to get every seed). Squeeze the garlic cloves out of their skins.
5. Purée the tomatoes, garlic, and stock in a food processor or blender. Season to taste with salt and pepper.
6. Serve the soup at room temperature. Garnish with plenty of chervil.

SERVES 8

This soup is fast and easy and one of my favorites. I make it all the time at home. The ingredients sound a little strange—cucumber and lettuce served hot? Trust me. In addition to tasting very fresh and clean, this is the perfect soup if you are watching your weight. In my line of work, I constantly struggle to keep my weight under control. My sister-in-law is a yoga instructor, and people always invite her for physical activities—hiking, swimming. With me, people think food. I am always invited to partake in food-related events: "You must try Aunt Nettie's nine-cheese-and-sausage lasagna!" This soup has saved me.

The tofu will add protein if you're making it as a "be good" soup. A fancier variation would be to omit the tofu and add a heavy dash of heavy cream; for quick dinner party fare, I add the cream.

2 medium onions or 1 leek, chopped
2 cloves garlic, minced
2 tablespoons extra-virgin olive oil
1 tablespoon butter (optional)
1/2 bunch celery with leaves, chopped
2 large cucumbers, peeled, cut length-
    wise in half, seeded, and cut into
    1/4-inch cubes (see Note)
1 head romaine lettuce, washed well and
    chopped
1 bunch watercress or arugula, washed
    well and chopped
4 good-quality vegetable bouillon cubes
    (see Note)
2 1/2 tablespoons minced fresh or dried
    savory
One 16-ounce package extra firm tofu,
    cut into cubes (optional)
Salt and cracked pepper to taste
Grated good-quality Pecorino Romano
    cheese

1. In a large heavy stockpot over low heat, sauté the onions and garlic in the olive oil and butter, if using, until the onions are translucent. Stir them frequently so they don't brown.
2. Add the celery and cucumbers and cook, stirring, until they start to soften. Cover all with water. (I use spring water.) Add the romaine and watercress.
3. Mince or crush the bouillon cubes and add them to the pot. (The soup does not simmer for long, so the bouillon may not have time to dissolve.) Add the

savory, tofu, if using, salt, and pepper. Let the soup simmer for about 5 minutes (if it cooks much longer the vegetables will get mushy). Serve with the Pecorino Romano cheese.

Note: Four small unwaxed Kirby cucumbers can be used instead of the two larger ones. They only need to be seeded; their skins can stay on.

Note: I use Morga bouillon cubes. They are a little pricey but worth it. Or maybe it's my local health food store that's pricey?

Coco's Louisiana Oyster and Chive Soup

Coco calls this soup her secret weapon; it's very quick and easy to make. It has a rich, complex, and elegant flavor but is light and not filling, the perfect start to a dinner party, with a glass of dry Champagne or sparkling wine. Of course, shucking your own oysters is optimal for freshness but, to make this dish even more simple to prepare, fresh shucked oysters can be purchased at most upscale supermarkets.

8 shucked large oysters (if you shuck your
   own oysters, add an extra 1/4 cup clam
   juice)
1/4 cup finely chopped fresh chives, or
   4 scallions, chopped
4 tablespoons (1/2 stick) butter
1/2 cup bottled clam juice (half an 8-ounce
   bottle)
1 3/4 cups whole milk
Salt and cracked pepper to taste

1. Place the oysters with their juice in a large bowl. Chop the oysters in the bottom of the bowl so as not to lose any of the juice.
2. In a heavy saucepan, simmer the chives in the butter over low heat for about 5 minutes.
3. Add the clam juice and simmer for another 5 minutes.
4. Bring the clam juice to a rolling boil, add the oysters, and remove from the heat. Let the soup cool down a bit, then slowly whisk in the milk. (This keeps the milk from separating.) When it is time to serve the soup, bring it back to a gentle simmer to warm it and season with salt and pepper to taste.

I am an avid fan of cabbage. My Hungarian grandfather always made some sort of cabbage dish when he came to visit, and I loved it. This soup is not at all heavy, so one can dip into it repeatedly free of caloric guilt. It tastes even better a day or two after making it.

2 onions, minced
8 cloves garlic, minced
3 tablespoons olive oil
2 green bell peppers, chopped
1 head green cabbage, cut in half, cored,
    and cut into thick ribbons
2 pounds lean top round beef, cut into
    1-inch cubes (optional)
4 fresh ripe tomatoes, cored, or canned
    Italian plum tomatoes, cut into large
    pieces
2 quarts V8 juice
¼ cup balsamic vinegar
3 tablespoons packed brown sugar
2 tablespoons Worcestershire
Salt and cracked pepper to taste

1. In a heavy stockpot over medium heat, sauté the onions and garlic in the olive oil until they are translucent. Add the green peppers, and sauté for 2 to 3 minutes. Add the cabbage and cook, stirring frequently, for another 2 to 3 minutes.
2. If you are adding the beef, brown the cubed pieces in a dash of olive oil in a skillet before adding them to the soup.
3. Add the beef, if using, and the remaining ingredients to the stockpot. Simmer over low heat for at least 1 hour.

SERVES 4

This may be one of my favorite recipes of all time. While it is quick and easy to prepare, the many different textures of this soup—from the crunch of the toast and fresh cilantro to the soft, smooth poached egg—combined with the sharp flavors of the paprika and fresh crushed garlic make it unusual and exceptional. This recipe calls for unsalted chicken broth because most conventional brands contain so much salt that after you add the other spices the soup is too salty. When I made this with regular broth, four out of my eight guests found the soup too salty.

Three 14½-ounce cans unsalted chicken
   broth or 6 cups chicken or vegetable
   stock (page 67 or 65)
1½ teaspoons sweet Hungarian paprika
¼ teaspoon cayenne pepper
Salt and cracked pepper to taste
2 to 3 cloves garlic, crushed through a
   garlic press
¼ cup chopped fresh cilantro, plus small
   sprigs for garnish
2 tablespoons extra-virgin olive oil
8 slices good-quality peasant, sour-
   dough, or wheat bread
1 to 2 tablespoons butter
4 large eggs
Parsley sprigs for garnish

1. Pour the broth into a stockpot and add the paprika, cayenne, salt, and pepper. Simmer over low heat.
2. Mix the crushed garlic with the cilantro and olive oil. Divide this mixture among 4 individual bowls.
3. In a skillet, brown the bread in a small amount of butter on both sides. Place 2 small slices or 1 large slice cut in half in each bowl.
4. Lightly poach the eggs as directed for Poached Eggs (page 20). The yolks should be left runny, as the hot chicken stock will cook the eggs a bit more. Place an egg in each bowl and ladle the hot broth over it. Garnish with sprigs of fresh cilantro and parsley. Serve immediately.

SERVES 8

This dish makes a delicious meal when served with guacamole or sliced avocado, warm fresh corn tortillas, and a huge tossed salad.

2 large boneless, skinless chicken breast
  halves
3 tablespoons olive oil
1 large Spanish onion, minced
5 cloves garlic, minced
2 fresh poblano peppers, chopped
8 ounces good-quality cured chorizo,
  sliced and chopped in quarters
1/4 teaspoon crushed red pepper flakes
8 cups chicken stock, homemade
  (page 67) or canned
Two 10-ounce bags good-quality frozen
  corn, or 4 cups fresh corn kernels
Salt and cracked pepper to taste
1/4 bunch cilantro, stems trimmed, minced
1 bunch radishes, trimmed and sliced
Queso fresco, crème fraîche, or sour
  cream

1. In a heavy stockpot over medium to low heat, cook the chicken breasts on both sides in half the olive oil. Remove the chicken and allow to cool. Add the remaining olive oil to the pot and heat it. Add the onion, garlic, poblanos, chorizo, and red pepper flakes. Sauté until the onion is soft and translucent. Add the chicken stock and bring to a boil.

2. Shred the chicken and add it to the boiling stock. Reduce the heat and simmer for 15 minutes. Add the corn, cook for about 2 minutes, and turn off the heat. Season the stew to taste with salt and pepper. Ladle the stew into bowls and garnish with the cilantro, radishes, and queso fresco.

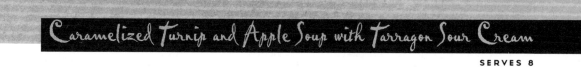

Caramelized Turnip and Apple Soup with Tarragon Sour Cream

This soup is very rich in flavor but at the same time light and not filling. The earthy taste of turnips combines well with the tartness of apples. The tarragon sour cream makes a strong flavor complement. Chicken stock can be substituted for water.

At Pongo we put the sour cream in a squeeze bottle and make designs with it on the top of the soup, as the soup is thick enough for the sour cream to stay in place. The soup alone, however, is creamy enough. Those who don't eat dairy can simply garnish the soup with minced tarragon and lemon zest.

1 large Spanish onion, cut in half through
    the root end, then cut into half-moon
    slices
7 cups chopped purple turnips (unpeeled)
3 Granny Smith apples, cored and chopped
1/4 cup olive oil
1 tablespoon fresh thyme leaves, plus
    small thyme sprigs for garnish
1 cup sour cream
1 1/2 tablespoons minced fresh tarragon
1 teaspoon grated lemon zest
Salt and cracked pepper

1. In a heavy stockpot over low heat, slowly cook the onion, turnips, and apples in the olive oil until they are soft and browned, stirring occasionally, about 35 to 45 minutes. Add the thyme and enough water to just cover the vegetables. Simmer covered over low heat for about 1 hour. If the soup is too thick, you can add a little more water. Let the soup cool a little.

2. In a small bowl, combine the sour cream, tarragon, and lemon zest.

3. Purée the soup in a blender or food processor, reheat, add salt and pepper to taste, and serve. Garnish with the tarragon sour cream and thyme sprigs.

SERVES 6

This soup has a rich, creamy texture and elaborate flavor with virtually no fat. It is vegetarian, but chicken stock can be substituted for water. It's dairy-free if you skip the mascarpone garnish, and it can be served hot or cold. I usually serve it with Spinach Salad with Grilled Red Onion Vinaigrette (page 95) for lunch or a light dinner.

> 3 medium white onions or 4 leeks, white parts only, minced
> 1 tablespoon extra-virgin olive oil
> 4 medium Idaho potatoes, peeled and cubed
> 4 cloves garlic, smashed and peeled
> 4 red bell peppers, roasted and peeled (page 221)
> 3 tablespoons dry white vermouth
> Salt and cracked black pepper to taste
> 2 tablespoons minced fresh sage
> Juice of 1/2 lemon
> 6 ounces mascarpone cheese
> Minced red bell pepper and small sage leaves for garnish

1. In a heavy stockpot over medium heat, sauté the onions in the olive oil until translucent but not brown. Add the potatoes, garlic, and water to cover; simmer covered until the potatoes are soft.

2. Purée this mixture with its liquid and the roasted red peppers in a blender or food processor. Strain the soup to remove any bits of skin or seeds, using a spoon or ladle to push the soup through the strainer. Discard what's left. Stir the vermouth into the soup. Season with salt and pepper to taste. If the soup is too thick, you can add a little more water. Either chill the soup or reheat it over low heat.

3. Mix the minced sage and lemon juice into the mascarpone cheese. Garnish the soup with a scoop of this mixture in each bowl; you may also garnish with a little minced red pepper and a sage leaf.

Saffron Mussel Bisque

This soup is complicated but well worth the effort. For a celebration, I would serve this with sparkling dry wine or Champagne. Farm-raised mussels are far less sandy than those from the ocean. I find farm-raised mussels much easier to work with, but the ocean variety often have a stronger flavor.

4 pounds mussels, small to medium in size,
  cleaned and debearded
1 tablespoon butter
1 tablespoon all-purpose flour
1 cup half-and-half or heavy cream
8 cups fish stock (page 46)
Salt and cracked pepper to taste
1 cup dry white wine of a quality you
  wouldn't mind drinking
2 small carrots, peeled and finely diced
1/2 teaspoon well-packed saffron threads
Parsley sprigs or minced fresh chives for
  garnish

1. Scrub the mussels in cold water, throwing away any that are open, and remove the beards.
2. In a small saucepan over low heat, melt the butter and whisk in the flour. Heat until bubbling. Pour in the half-and-half and cook, whisking, until thickened. Remove from the heat.
3. In a pot large enough to hold the stock and mussels, bring the stock to a medium boil. Have another medium-sized pot and large strainer ready.
4. Drop the mussels into the boiling stock, cover, and cook just until they open. Immediately pour the mussels and broth through the strainer into the medium-size pot. *Do not discard the stock.* Let the mussels cool, then shuck them and chill until you are ready to serve. Leave a few mussels in their shells to put on top of the soup when it is served.
5. Strain the stock that the mussels have cooked in through a strainer lined with cheesecloth or a coffee filter. Rinse out the medium-sized pot, return the stock to it, and season with salt and pepper.
6. Whisk the white wine, carrots, saffron, and cream mixture into the stock and bring to a slow boil. Simmer over very low heat for 30 to 45 minutes. Stir in the shucked mussels and simmer for 1 minute. Do not overcook or the mussels will become tough. Garnish with the mussels in their shells and the parsley sprigs.

They say that smell and taste memories are more intense and long-lasting than those of sight. This dish takes me back to when I was twelve years old and living in Sevilla, Spain. After school I would often go to our neighborhood café (the Bar Philapinas in the Barrio Santa Cruz) to eat this soup. The same waiter was still there ten years later when I went back, and he was still wearing the same double-breasted white jacket with silver buttons. When I walked into the bar, he smiled with recognition and said, *"¿Un potaje de garbanzo?"*

The original dish is made with tripe and seasoned rendered pork fat, but we don't need to be *that* authentic.

As you eat this soup, spoon the soft garlic out of its skin. Spread the sweet cloves on toast or mix them in the soup. The garlic skins will be all that's left in the bottom of the bowl.

8 slices bacon
3 whole garlic bulbs, cut horizontally in
   half, skins intact
6 medium Idaho or Yukon Gold potatoes,
   peeled and coarsely chopped
2 tablespoons good-quality Hungarian
   paprika
10 cups chicken stock, homemade
   (page 67) or canned
Three 19-ounce cans chickpeas, drained
   and rinsed
Extra-virgin olive oil for garnish
Salt and cracked pepper to taste

1. Cut the bacon into quarters while it is still cold. In a heavy stockpot over medium-low heat, brown the bacon. Remove the bacon, leaving the fat in the stockpot.
2. Lay the garlic bulbs flat side down in the hot fat and sauté them slowly until they are golden brown. If they become too dark, the soup will be bitter. Remove the halved garlic bulbs and reserve.
3. Add the potatoes to the bacon fat and brown them until they are just starting to stick. Reduce the heat and add the paprika. Stir the potatoes and continue to cook until they are slightly browned and evenly coated with the paprika, about 5 minutes.
4. Cover the potatoes with the chicken stock and add the chickpeas. Return the

garlic and bacon to the pot. Simmer the soup over low heat until thickened, 45 minutes to 1 hour. Serve with a little olive oil drizzled on top and season with salt and cracked pepper. Be sure to also serve an outstanding crusty bread and a Spanish Rioja or other fruity red wine.

SERVES 8

This stew is an intricate combination of textures and flavors. It has a deep jade green color and gets better spoonful after spoonful. It is an excellent meal paired with a big salad and crispy chicken and queso tacos. I cut the tacos in half and use them as a garnish in the soup. The crunch of the tacos is so good with the stew. Or skip the tacos and simply garnish the soup with shredded chicken, fried tortilla strips, and cheese. If you're vegetarian, omit the chicken. The tortillas and cheese are great by themselves.

2 dozen medium tomatillos, husked and
    well rinsed
2 tablespoons olive oil
3 poblano peppers, roasted and peeled
    (see page 221)
1/4 bunch cilantro, stemmed and coarsely
    chopped, plus small sprigs for garnish
1 bunch scallions, chopped
8 cloves garlic, coarsely sliced
1 large Spanish onion or 3 medium onions,
    minced
1/2 bunch celery, minced
3 fresh poblano peppers, chopped
1 tablespoon ground cumin
2 teaspoons chopped fresh or dried
    oregano
4 cups chicken or vegetable stock, home-
    made (page 67 or 65) or canned
2 teaspoons sugar
3 cups canned whole-kernel hominy,
    drained and rinsed
Salt and cracked pepper to taste
2 cups shredded Mexican or Armenian
    string cheese (see Note)
2 cups shredded cooked chicken breast
10 to 12 good-quality fresh yellow or blue
    corn tortillas

1. Preheat the broiler. Heat a large cast-iron skillet under the broiler. Drop in the tomatillos and 1 tablespoon of the olive oil and stir to coat. Broil the tomatillos, turning them frequently, until they are browned on both sides and look a bit deflated. Purée them with the roasted poblano peppers, the cilantro, and scallions in a food processor or blender.

2. In a large heavy soup pot over medium heat, sauté the garlic, onion, celery,

fresh poblano peppers, cumin, and oregano in the remaining tablespoon of olive oil until the vegetables are lightly browned. Add the tomatillo purée and chicken stock. Bring to a medium boil and add the sugar and hominy. Add salt and cracked pepper to taste and simmer for another 5 minutes.

3. For each serving, sprinkle shredded string cheese and chicken on a corn tortilla, top with another tortilla, and toast in a large cast-iron skillet or comal on both sides until the cheese has melted. Cut in half or quarters and serve the soup with the tacos sticking out of the soup. Or you can cut the tortillas in ¼-inch strips and fry them in 1 cup vegetable, peanut, or canola oil until they are crisp. Haystack the strips over a small handful of shredded chicken and another of string cheese on each serving. Another option is to warm the corn tortillas in a dry cast-iron skillet or comal, wrap them in a cloth napkin to keep them warm, and serve them alongside the soup. Any of these garnish options should include a few cilantro sprigs.

Note: Finding the right kind of string cheese may be a bit of a challenge but well worth the hunt. Any Mexican grocery or specialty store should carry it. It is sometimes referred to as Oaxacan string cheese. Italian string cheese tends to be a little bit more oily and is not bright white; Armenian string cheese is closer to the Mexican. If you can't find the Mexican or Armenian string cheeses, shredded fresh mozzarella can be substituted. If you do find a good supplier of Mexican products, stock up on good-quality corn tortillas and freeze them.

SERVES 8

While sitting at the bar of Café Pongo, Chris Mehan, our best examplar of local color, was paging through my cookbook notes when he noticed a recipe for African peanut soup in the table of contents. He leapt from his barstool and told me that just the night before he had been awakened in the middle of the night by a call from his friend Lauren Pickford. Lauren, a renowned New Orleans jazz musician, was calling to tell Chris about this amazing peanut soup he had just made with the guidance of some of the Africans in his band. Chris and I ran and gathered some collards and a jar of peanut butter and headed straight for his house. Just as our first bottle of wine was at an end, the kitchen was filling with the good smells of this soup. Lauren's CDs played the entire time. It was hard to say which was better, the jazz or the soup.

Soup:

3 medium yams, washed well, dried, and
   rubbed with oil
2 medium onions or 1 large, chopped
4 cloves garlic, minced
2 tablespoons olive oil
1 bunch collard greens, washed and sliced
   (7 cups well packed)
Four 14^{1}/$_2$-ounce cans chicken or
   vegetable stock or homemade
   (pages 67 and 65)
Three 28-ounce cans whole plum tomatoes,
   coarsely chopped, juice reserved
2 tablespoons balsamic vinegar
3 tablespoons crunchy peanut butter
2 tablespoons brown sugar
1 tablespoon fresh thyme leaves
1 tablespoon good-quality curry powder
^{1}/$_4$ teaspoon cayenne pepper
^{3}/$_4$ cup basmati rice

Garnish:

6 tablespoons coarsely chopped roasted
   peanuts
1 clove garlic, thinly sliced
1 tablespoon butter
1 teaspoon brown sugar
Dash of cayenne pepper

For the soup:

1. Preheat the oven to 400 degrees.
2. Bake the yams in the oven until they are soft all the way through, 30 to 45 minutes.
3. In a heavy stockpot over medium heat, sauté the onions and garlic in the olive oil until the onions are translucent. Add the collard greens and sauté until tender.
4. Add the stock, tomatoes with their juice, vinegar, peanut butter, brown sugar, thyme, curry powder, and cayenne. Simmer for about 15 minutes. Add the rice and continue to simmer for 12 to 15 minutes. Remove the soup from the heat and let it stand for another 5 minutes. *Do not overcook or the rice will become mushy.* Remember, the rice will continue to cook after it is removed from the heat. If the soup is too thick, add more stock or water.

For the garnish:

5. In a small skillet, toast the peanuts and garlic in the butter until the garlic is light golden brown. Add the sugar and cayenne and stir until the peanuts are well coated. Remove from the heat and set aside.

To finish the dish:

6. Cut the yams into quarters and divide them among the soup bowls. Ladle the soup over the yams. Sprinkle the sautéed peanuts over the top.

SERVES 6 TO 8

I've spent many memorable days at my friend Brian's small cottage in eastern New York, just across the border from Great Barrington, Massachusetts. Brian is an outstanding cook as well as a gardener. Many of my best recipes have been conceived at his house with herbs and vegetables from his garden, supplemented by provisions from Guido's in Great Barrington (quite possibly the best specialty food store on the eastern seaboard). On the weekends, Brian's spare rooms are almost always filled with guests, and there are always fresh flowers in every room. In winter the stone fireplace burns day and night. In summer we eat on the screened porch and look out on the mountains. Brian starts this stew Saturday night so that the flavors have time to sit and meld. On Sunday morning/afternoon, his guests drift in and out of the kitchen, shuffling in pajamas, filling and refilling their mugs and bowls.

2 large onions, diced
6 cloves garlic, crushed through a garlic press
2 tablespoons olive oil
2 good-sized boneless, skinless chicken breast halves, cut into large chunks
2 chicken leg quarters
3 carrots, peeled and sliced about 1/4 inch thick
10 medium-size red Bliss potatoes, scrubbed and cut into large cubes
Half 750-ml bottle red wine
1/4 cup tomato paste
One 15-ounce can beef stock
4 cups chicken stock, homemade (page 67) or canned
10 large mushroom caps, sliced
4 hearty sausages, sliced (a duck or pheasant sausage is nice if you can find it)
3 whole cloves
1 teaspoon whole peppercorns
4 bay leaves
Salt to taste
10 thyme sprigs, leaves removed

1. In a heavy stockpot over medium heat, sauté the onions and garlic in the olive oil until translucent. Add the chicken breast chunks and legs and

brown them on both sides. Add the carrots and potatoes and brown for 1 to 2 minutes.

2. Add the remaining ingredients except for half the thyme leaves and stir well. Bring to a boil, then simmer covered for at least 1 hour, stirring regularly. This stew can be prepared in advance (the longer it sits the more the flavors will meld together). Reheat it just before serving. Garnish by sprinkling the remaining thyme across the top of each bowl. Serve with crusty bread.

3
SALADS AND SANDWICHES

Although I consider myself an able cook, I was historically a bad salad maker. I suspect the problem was that I underestimated salad. I saw it as a trivial side dish. It wasn't until I ate the salads of a few masters that I began to catch on. Two things began my enlightenment, the first being the discovery of the salad spinner (an indispensable tool in the making of salad). The second was in 1984 when I first tried balsamic vinegar. Today these things do not seem like any big deal, but like most first-time experiences there is awe in the unknown.

I am now an avid salad maker. I enjoy eating salad *with*, rather than before or after, the meal. I love hot pasta next to a crisp salad; the sharp tang of the vinegar and the crunch of the greens combines well with the chewy slightly sweet flavor of the noodle. Texture and flavor contrasts are essential in good food—sweet hitting salty, crunch mixed with soft. Salad is an opportunity for all these elements to occur simultaneously and harmoniously.

Dressings are great, but once you get the proportions right, good old oil and vinegar is sometimes just the trick. I keep many vinegars on hand—balsamic, of course, but also sherry, white wine, rice wine, apple cider, and the standard red wine. Match the vinegar to the food, and the salad will be the perfect complement.

Café Pongo House Salad Dressing

YIELDS 1 CUP

Over the years many customers have asked for this recipe. At the restaurant, we use it to marinate mushrooms, sauté certain vegetables, splash on sandwiches, and marinate meats. I keep it in a squeeze bottle at home and am constantly finding new uses for it.

1/4 cup balsamic vinegar
3 tablespoons sugar
2 tablespoons Dijon mustard
1/2 teaspoon soy sauce
1/2 cup extra-virgin olive oil

1. In a food processor or blender or with a hand mixer, combine all the ingredients except for the olive oil.
2. With the machine running, very slowly drizzle in the olive oil and mix until it is fully combined. Enjoy on your favorite lettuce.

Ruby Grapefruit with Fresh Mint and Garam Masala

SERVES 2

This refreshing salad is perfect before or after a spicy meal, or to cleanse the palate between courses. The grapefruit must be perfectly sweet and juicy.

2 pink grapefruit, peel and pith removed,
  cut into bite-sized pieces (see Note)
6 fresh mint sprigs, stems removed,
  leaves cut into thin ribbons
1 teaspoon garam masala
3 tablespoons extra-virgin olive oil

Toss all the ingredients together and enjoy.

Note: For this type of salad, all the pith (the bitter white part between the skin and the fruit) must be removed. To do so, cut the top and bottom off the fruit, stand it up on a flat end, and slice along the outside, removing the white pith along with the peel. Cut into bite-sized pieces.

Honeydew and Red Onion Salad with Fresh Mint and Saga Blue Cheese

This cool and refreshing summer salad perfectly complements grilled fresh tuna, or even albacore tuna canned in spring water. The key to this salad is the ripe sweet melon. The smell of a melon even before it is cut is a good indicator of ripeness. If it feels soft at the navel and smells sweet, it is probably perfect.

1 large red onion, cut in half through the
  root end, then cut into ¼-inch half-
  moon slices
2 tablespoons extra-virgin olive oil
1 ripe honeydew melon, seeded, peeled,
  and cut into 1-inch cubes
Juice of 1 lime
6 fresh mint sprigs, stems removed,
  leaves cut into thin ribbons
2 tablespoons fresh basil leaves, cut into
  thin ribbons
4 to 8 tablespoons crumbled Saga or other
  Danish blue cheese
Dash of salt
Cracked pepper to taste

1. In a sauté pan over medium heat, sauté the onion in the olive oil just until it begins to soften. The onion is not being cooked but simply "sweated" to remove its bitterness.
2. Toss the honeydew with the lime juice. Add the onion and remaining ingredients and toss to combine. Serve immediately.

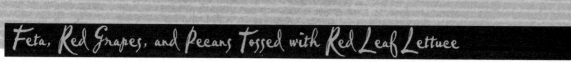
Feta, Red Grapes, and Pecans Tossed with Red Leaf Lettuce

Very quick, very simple, very tasty!

> 1 cup crumbled good-quality feta
> 2 cups halved and seeded red grapes
> 1 cup chopped pecans
> 1 head red leaf lettuce, washed, dried,
>   and torn into bite-sized pieces
> ½ cup extra-virgin olive oil
> ¼ cup balsamic vinegar
> Cracked pepper to taste

1. Combine the feta, grapes, and pecans together. Gently toss with the lettuce.
2. Whisk the oil and vinegar together. Dress the salad and toss. Serve immediately with cracked pepper on top.

SERVES 2 TO 4

When blood oranges are available, buy them first and think of uses for them later. They are as flavorful as they are beautiful. With the addition of a beautiful dark green, crisp bunch of watercress and a lemon you can make this salad. The combination of the sweet-and-sour citrus with the watercress is well suited for serving with grilled chicken or fish.

Juice of ½ Meyer lemon, or use ½ regular
   lemon with a dash of sugar
¼ cup fresh blood orange juice
½ cup extra-virgin olive oil
1 clove garlic, minced
Salt and cracked pepper to taste
1 bunch watercress, large stems trimmed,
   washed and dried

Whisk together the lemon and orange juices, olive oil, garlic, salt, and pepper. Toss with the watercress and serve immediately. Garnish with slices of blood oranges.

Spinach Salad with Grilled Red Onion Vinaigrette

The key to this salad is grilling the onion. The red onion vinaigrette is so good you may want to make extra. It also makes a great chicken and steak marinade, as well as an outstanding spinach salad.

This was the first recipe of Roland's I ever tasted. With this salad he was hired.

DRESSING:

1 medium red onion, peeled and cut in
  half through the root end
1/4 cup red wine vinegar
2 tablespoons sugar
1 1/2 tablespoons grainy mustard
3/4 cup extra-virgin olive oil
Salt and cracked pepper to taste

SALAD:

1 pound curly leaf spinach, stems
  removed, washed and dried (see Note)
3 hard-boiled eggs, peeled and chopped

FOR THE DRESSING:

1. Over a charcoal- or wood-fired grill, slowly grill the onion until it is blackened on both sides. If you can't get to a grill, heat a cast-iron skillet over medium heat until it is just starting to smoke and blacken the onion in the skillet. Turn your exhaust fan on high. Let the onion cool.

2. Cut the onion lengthwise in thin slices and put them in a bowl. Whisk the remaining dressing ingredients together and pour over the onion. Let sit at least 1 hour.

FOR THE SALAD:

3. Just before serving, toss the spinach with the egg and the red onion vinaigrette.

Note: When you are washing a particularly gritty green like spinach or arugula, you must submerged it in at least 4 inches of water. This way the grit will drop to the bottom, and the greens can then be lifted out of the water and spun dry. If the water is simply run over the greens in a colander, the grit settles right back on them.

SERVES 4

This salad is crisp and tangy. The warm lentil croutons soak up a little of the dressing when they are tossed into the salad, making them truly divine. This is the kind of salad that makes you want to take the whole serving bowl with a fork and wander out to the garden to eat slowly.

CROUTONS:

8 ounces dried brown lentils
1 tablespoon minced garlic
2 tablespoons minced fresh ginger
8 scallions, thinly sliced
2 tablespoons minced fresh cilantro
2 teaspoons baking powder
Dash of cayenne pepper
1 teaspoon salt
2 cups vegetable, peanut, or canola oil

DRESSING:

Grated zest of 1 lemon
Juice of 2 1/2 lemons
1/4 cup tahini (sesame seed paste)
1/4 cup soy sauce
3 tablespoons red wine vinegar
1 cup extra-virgin olive oil
1 teaspoon sugar
1/2 teaspoon cayenne pepper

SALAD:

4 romaine hearts, torn into bite-sized
   pieces
3 ripe tomatoes, chopped
1 cucumber, chopped

FOR THE CROUTONS:
1. Soak the lentils in water to cover for about 8 hours, changing the water a few times.
2. Drain the lentils, pat them dry, and put them in a food processor or blender. Combine the garlic, ginger, scallions, cilantro, baking powder, cayenne, and salt. Add this mixture to the lentils and purée until smooth. Form the mixture into 1-inch patties.

FOR THE DRESSING:
3. In a food processor or blender, process all the ingredients until smooth.

4. Heat the oil for the croutons in a deep, heavy skillet over medium heat. Add as many of the croutons as will fit in a single layer and fry on all sides until golden brown. Dry on paper towels. The croutons should be served hot.

FOR THE SALAD:

5. Toss the romaine, tomatoes, and cucumbers with the hot croutons and two-thirds of the dressing. Serve immediately with the remaining dressing on the side.

This salad is beautiful in color as well as flavor.

DRESSING:

¼ cup balsamic vinegar
3 tablespoons sugar
2 tablespoons Dijon mustard
½ teaspoon soy sauce
½ cup extra-virgin olive oil

SALAD:

2 ripe Anjou, Bartlett, or red pears
Juice of ½ lemon
1 large head Bibb lettuce, washed, dried,
    and torn into bite-sized pieces
2 to 3 ounces good-quality Stilton cheese
Seeds of 1 pomegranate

FOR THE DRESSING:

1. In a food processor or blender or with a hand mixer, combine all the ingredients except for the olive oil.
2. With the machine running, very slowly drizzle in the olive oil and mix until fully combined.

FOR THE SALAD:

3. Cut the "cheeks" off the pears, bypassing their cores. Lay the pear cheeks on their flat sides and cut into thin slices. These halves can be fanned out like a deck of cards for an attractive presentation. Cut the remaining fruit from the sides of the core, lay those pieces skin side up, and slice them. You will have perfect uniform slices.
4. Squeeze the lemon juice over the pear slices.
5. Mound the Bibb lettuce on 2 plates. Arrange the sliced pear halves on the side of each plate. Drizzle the desired amount of salad dressing over the lettuce. Crumble the Stilton and strew additional pear slices over the top of the dressed lettuce. Sprinkle the pomegranate seeds over the entire plate.

SERVES 2

This salad has been on our menu since we opened. The warm dressing softens the blue cheese and melts with the sweetness of the caramelized onions. Serve it with a warm crispy baguette.

> 6 cups mesclun greens, washed and dried
> 4 to 6 tablespoons crumbled blue cheese
>   (a Danish blue works well)
> 4 to 6 tablespoons walnut pieces
> 1 to 2 onions, caramelized (page 137)
> 1/4 to 1/2 cup Café Pongo House Salad
>   Dressing (page 91)

1. Divide the greens between 2 individual plates, then divide the blue cheese, walnuts, and caramelized onions between the salads.
2. Put the desired amount of dressing into a small saucepan and heat the dressing until just before it begins to boil (if you overheat the dressing it will "break").
3. Pour equal amounts of dressing over the salads and serve immediately.

The idea for this salad was inspired by a similar dish served at Philadelphia's White Dog Café. As a Philly native who visits often, I have enjoyed the creative kitchen of the White Dog for many years. Roland and I had an immediate connection when I first found out that he had been the *chef de cuisine* there. We both have tremendous respect and admiration for that business as well for its chef/owner Kevin Von Claus, whose innovative recipes never cease to inspire me.

This salad is beautiful to serve. It is a great salad for dinner parties because it is easily prepared ahead of time and is a welcome departure from the usual tossed salad. The dressing can also be used with a wide variety of greens. The soft favor of the rosemary mixes well with the flowery citrus flavor of the clementines.

SALAD:

4 large or 6 small beets
1 bulb fennel
Cracked black pepper to taste

DRESSING:

1/2 cup extra-virgin olive oil
Grated zest of 1 clementine
Juice of 3 clementines
4 teaspoons rice wine vinegar
1 tablespoon minced fresh rosemary, plus
   4 teaspoons rosemary leaves for
   garnish
1/2 teaspoon grated lemon zest

FOR THE SALAD:

1. Rinse the beets, put them in a pan with water to cover, and boil covered until they can be stabbed somewhat easily with a fork. Drain them and cool under cold running water. As the water is running, you can rub off the peels and stems of the beets. This will dye your hands red, but it is quick and easy. Slice the beets very thin and refrigerate them.

2. Trim any discolored outer parts from the fennel. Trim the tops and the base. Using a mandoline, shave the fennel crosswise in almost paper thin slices. If you don't have a mandoline cut the fennel lengthwise in half, lay the halves down on their flat sides, and slice crosswise as thin as possible. Soak the fennel in ice water while you prepare the dressing.

FOR THE DRESSING:

3. Whisk together all the ingredients.

TO FINISH THE DISH:

4. On 4 salad plates, arrange the beet slices so they are covering the bottom of the plates. Shake the water off a tuft of fennel and place it on top of the beets. Sprinkle about 4 teaspoon fresh rosemary needles on top of each salad.
5. Pour the dressing over the chilled salads. Crack the pepper over each plate at the table.

This is a hipper, sexier version of the original.

2 tablespoons olive oil
Salt and cracked pepper to taste
4 small or 2 huge whole chicken breasts,
   skinned and boned
1 cup chopped walnuts
1 cup red grapes, halved and seeded
1/4 cup mayonnaise
1 tablespoon Dijon mustard
1 tablespoon minced fresh rosemary
3 tablespoons minced fresh parsley
1 teaspoon minced fresh tarragon
1/2 teaspoon minced fresh sage
1 large head red leaf lettuce, washed,
   dried, and torn into bite-sized pieces
1 bunch watercress, large stems trimmed,
   washed and dried
1 lemon, cut into wedges
Small fresh herb sprigs for garnish

1. Preheat the oven to 400 degrees.
2. Rub the olive oil, salt, and pepper over the chicken breasts, put them in a baking pan, and bake until the chicken is no longer pink at the center, 25 to 35 minutes. Check the chicken by cutting into it—remember, it's going to be cut up anyway. Allow the chicken to cool in its juices. Trim the center cartilage from between the breasts, cut the chicken into ½-inch cubes, and chill.
3. Combine the chilled chicken, the walnuts, grapes, mayonaise, mustard, rosemary, parsley, tarragon, and sage. Divide the red leaf lettuce and watercress among 4 to 6 plates. Scoop the chicken salad onto each plate. Garnish with the lemon wedges and herb sprigs. If additional dressing is desired, drizzle with Café Pongo House Salad Dressing (page 91).

Crusted Rare Tuna over Greens with Ginger-Horseradish Vinaigrette

SERVES 2

This is a light lunch salad, a perfect meal for those watching their carbohydrate intake (it's so satisfying that the carbs will not be missed). The tuna is crusted in Eden Shake, which is available at most health food stores. If it cannot be found the two most important ingredients are sesame seeds and nori flakes. Nori is the seaweed that sushi is wrapped in and is sold in sheets (for sushi) as well as flakes. Crumble the sheets into a food processor, pulse lightly, and, presto, you've got nori flakes.

1/2 cup extra-virgin olive oil
1/4 cup rice wine vinegar
1/2 teaspoon toasted sesame oil
1 tablespoon brown sugar
1 tablespoon minced fresh ginger
1/2 teaspoon chili oil
1 tablespoon (packed) minced fresh basil
1 tablespoon horseradish, or 1 teaspoon wasabi paste
Salt and cracked pepper to taste
1/4 cup Eden Shake or equal part sesame seeds and nori flakes

Two 1-inch-thick very fresh, sushi-grade tuna steaks, 6 to 8 ounces each
Cooking spray
1 bunch or combination of the following greens: red leaf lettuce, watercress, frisée, mizuna, or chicory, washed, dried, and torn into bite-sized pieces
1 cucumber, peeled, seeded, and sliced

1. Whisk together the olive oil, vinegar, sesame oil, brown sugar, ginger, chili oil, basil, horseradish, salt, and pepper. Pour into a jar.
2. Pour the Eden Shake onto a plate. Press the tuna steaks into the Eden Shake, coating all sides except one flat side.
3. Spray a sauté pan with cooking spray and heat over high heat. Place the tuna steaks bare side down in the pan and sear until the underside is brown, 1 to 2 minutes. Turn the steaks over and lightly brown the seeded side. (A rare steak is seared golden brown on one side and just lightly cooked on the other. A well-done fillet is flipped back and forth.) The tuna should remain totally pink on the inside. Remember, you could eat the tuna raw. Searing just crisps the outside and adds color. If you cook the fish through, it is a waste of quality tuna; you may as well serve Chicken of the Sea.
4. Carefully cut the tuna steaks into 1/4-inch-thick slices.
5. Divide the greens between 2 plates. Fan the tuna slices over the greens and arrange the cucumber slices around the tuna. Shake the dressing well, dress the salads, and serve.

Salads and Sandwiches 103

Salad of Filet Mignon, Arugula, and Red-Wine-Sautéed Mushrooms

This salad is very satisfying, yet remarkably low in fat—a perfect meal for those watching their carbohydrate and fat intake. It is quick and easy to prepare.

> 1 tablespoon kosher salt
> 2 filet mignon steaks, 6 to 8 ounces each
> 1 tablespoon extra-virgin olive oil
> 1 Vidalia onion, minced
> 1 tablespoon fresh thyme leaves, or
>   1 teaspoon dried
> Fresh cracked pepper—*lots of it!*
> 1 1/2 cups red wine
> 10 ounces white mushrooms, trimmed and
>   cut into quarters
> 1 head red leaf lettuce, washed, dried,
>   and torn into bite-sized pieces
> 1 small bunch arugula, large stems
>   trimmed, washed and dried

1. Sprinkle the kosher salt in a cast-iron skillet and heat the skillet over high heat until it is smoking. Press the steaks into the salt on the bottom of the pan and sear them on one side. Turn the steaks over and cook until the steak is done to your liking. (A rare steak is seared crisp on one side and just lightly cooked on the other. A well-done steak is flipped back and forth.) Remove the steaks from the pan and reduce the heat. Drop in the olive oil, onion, thyme, and cracked pepper. Cook until the onion begins to brown.

2. Pour the red wine over the onion and add the mushrooms. Simmer over low heat, stirring occasionally, until most of the liquid is absorbed, 3 to 5 minutes.

3. While the mushrooms are simmering, slice the steak and divide the greens between 2 plates.

4. Ladle the warm mushrooms over the greens. Arrange the sliced steak over the mushrooms. Sprinkle with more cracked pepper.

SANDWICHES

The way a sandwich is assembled is key to how good it tastes. The secret to achieving excellence is getting the correct ratio of wet to dry. A great sandwich is never dry (too bready). At Pongo we pull out and discard all the soft white centers from our delicious baguettes. What is left are two canoe-shaped halves. This hollowed-out bread is then packed full with any number of ingredients and doused with a generous splash of our house dressing. Closing a Pongo sandwich is like shutting an overpacked suitcase. Assembly is crucial to the creation of the perfect sandwich.

Pongo's World-Famous BLT

So simple, and yet so many subtle differences transform "good" to "world's best." Be sure to read the introduction to sandwich making (page 106) and follow the assembly procedures.

> 1 good-quality fresh baguette, split lengthwise in half but not separated, soft centers removed
> 5 tablespoons Hellmann's mayonnaise, or aioli (page 119) made without the red peppers
> 3 tablespoons fresh basil pesto (page 31)
> 10 slices bacon, cooked until crisp
> 2 large or 4 small good-quality tomatoes, preferably beefsteak
> 3 to 4 tablespoons Café Pongo House Salad Dressing (page 91)
> 1 large head red leaf lettuce, leaves separated, washed, and dried

1. Under a broiler or on a griddle, lightly toast the inside of the baguette.
2. Combine the mayonnaise and pesto. Spread the pesto mayonnaise all over the inside of both halves of the baguette.
3. Lay the bacon along the length of the bottom half of the bread. Lay the tomato slices on top of the bacon and drizzle with the house dressing. Fill the remaining cavity with the lettuce leaves. Close the sandwich tightly. Cut on a diagonal with a sharp serrated knife into 2 to 4 pieces. You may need toothpicks to keep the sandwiches together.

SERVES 4 TO 6

This simple recipe has been a standard since the day we opened, and we are still being complimented on its tastiness. Seven years later it is still our best-selling sandwich.

2 tablespoons extra-virgin olive oil
Salt and cracked pepper to taste
4 small or 2 huge whole chicken breasts, skinned and boned
3 tablespoons pesto (page 30)
3 tablespoons Hellmann's mayonnaise or aioli (page 119) made without the red peppers
2 tablespoons fresh lemon juice
1 tablespoon Dijon mustard
2 tablespoons minced fresh tarragon, or 1 tablespoon dried
2 baguettes, split lengthwise in half but not separated, soft centers removed
2 ripe tomatoes or roasted and peeled red peppers (page 221), sliced
1 head red leaf lettuce, leaves separated, or 4 cups mesclun greens, washed and dried
2 to 4 tablespoons Café Pongo House Salad Dressing (page 91)

1. Preheat the oven to 400 degrees.
2. Rub the olive oil, salt, and pepper over the chicken breasts, put them in a baking pan, and bake until the chicken is no longer pink at the center, about 25 to 35 minutes. Check the chicken by cutting into it—it's going to be cut up anyway. Allow the chicken to cool in its juices. Trim the center cartilage from between the breasts, cut the chicken into ½-inch cubes, and chill.
3. Combine the chilled chicken, pesto, mayonnaise, lemon juice, mustard, and tarragon.
4. Under a broiler or on a griddle, lightly toast the insides of the baguettes.
5. Scoop the chicken salad into half of each baguette and cover with tomato slices. Divide the lettuce between the other halves of the baguettes and drizzle with the house dressing. Close the sandwiches tightly. Cut each sandwich on the diagonal with a sharp serrated knife into 2 or 3 pieces. You may need toothpicks to keep the sandwiches together.

Mushrooms on Multigrain Walnut Bread with Blue Cheese and Roasted Red Peppers

We can't expect everyone to bake bread for their sandwiches from scratch. At Pongo we are spoiled by Mikee, who bakes heavenly bread every day, but this sandwich *really* is good on our multigrain walnut bread. It has been so long since I've tasted anyone else's bread that I have a hard time fathoming a substitution. Nevertheless if your local bakery makes a good multigrain bread—*with walnuts*—then it can be substituted for ours.

> 2 cups thick-sliced portobello and
>   assorted mushrooms
> 1/2 cup Café Pongo House Salad Dressing
>   (page 91)
> 2 red bell peppers, roasted, peeled, and
>   cut into strips (page 221)
> 2 to 4 tablespoons crumbled blue cheese
>   (see Note)
> Four 1/2-inch-thick slices Multigrain
>   Walnut Bread (page 263)

1. Sauté the mushrooms in the dressing until they have soaked up ample amounts of it. Add the red peppers to the mushrooms just long enough for them to heat up. Spread the blue cheese on one side of 2 slices of the bread and divide the mushrooms and peppers over the blue cheese. Cover with the remaining bread.

2. In a skillet or on a griddle over medium-low heat, toast the sandwiches on both sides as you would a grilled cheese sandwich. There is no need for butter. The sandwiches are ready when they are golden brown on both sides.

Note: The blue cheese is easier to spread if it is quickly zapped in the microwave.

Artichoke Pesto Wraps with Goat Cheese, Sautéed Zucchini, and Roasted Red Peppers

The soft flavor of the goat cheese, combined with the zucchini and peppers, is perfect with this artichoke pesto. The pesto can also be served as a dip, with ½ cup chopped red bell peppers added for color.

ARTICHOKE PESTO:

1 cup unseasoned bottled or canned
   artichoke hearts, cut in half
4 tablespoons extra-virgin olive oil
½ cup grated Parmesan cheese
¼ cup chopped walnuts
3 cloves garlic, minced
¼ bunch parsley, stems removed, leaves minced
2 tablespoons minced fresh basil
1 tablespoon fresh thyme leaves
1 tablespoon red wine vinegar
Pinch of sugar

WRAPS:

2 medium zucchini, cut into ¼-inch-thick slices
2 tablespoons extra-virgin olive oil
4 to 6 large flour tortillas
2 red bell peppers, roasted, peeled, and
   cut into thick strips (page 221)
½ cup goat cheese
Salt and cracked pepper to taste

FOR THE ARTICHOKE PESTO:

1. In a sauté pan over medium heat, brown one side of the artichokes in 1 to 2 tablespoons of the olive oil. Let cool. In a blender or food processor, lightly purée the artichokes. Add the remaining ingredients and process just until combined.

FOR THE WRAPS:

2. In a sauté pan over medium heat, sauté the zucchini in the olive oil until it has some color.
3. Directly over a medium gas flame or in a heavy cast-iron skillet or comal, using tongs, warm the flour tortillas on both sides; they will rise with pockets of warm air.
4. Fill the center of each tortilla with some of the pesto, zucchini, red peppers, and goat cheese. Season with salt and pepper. Roll up, slice on a diagonal, and enjoy.

Wilted Spinach Sandwich with Caramelized Onions, Tomatoes, and Melted Cheddar

This is a very cozy sandwich, warm and soothing, and much healthier than, say, a meatball Parmesan sub. People travel from near and far for this famed sandwich.

1/2 baguette
2 to 3 tablespoons extra-virgin olive oil
4 cloves garlic, minced
8 ounces fresh spinach, stems removed, washed, and dried
2 tablespoons Caramelized Onions (page 137)
2 canned or fresh plum tomatoes, chopped, or 1/2 cup fresh salsa, well drained
2 or 3 slices Cheddar cheese, or enough grated Cheddar to cover

1. Split the baguette lengthwise but don't separate the halves. This way you can bite into the finished sandwich without hot liquid spurting out and burning your fingers. Pull the soft centers from the bread and sprinkle the remaining baguette with 1 tablespoon of the olive oil and half the garlic (or more if you like). Under the broiler, toast the inside of the bread until golden brown.

2. In a sauté pan over medium heat, lightly sauté the spinach with the remaining olive oil and garlic. Fill both sides of the bread with the spinach, layer on the onions and tomatoes, then top with the cheese. Toast the sandwich open faced under the broiler until the cheese is golden brown.

SERVES 6 TO 8

This recipe started out as our veggie burger but quickly evolved into fritters, too—the only difference being the size of the patty. This version of the recipe evolved because I noticed we were throwing out large quantities of portobello mushroom stems. I used them for soup stocks, but there would always be more. Heather, a friend and waitress, made a sautéed veggie burger on a slow night, and we adapted her recipe. I thought the toughness of portobello stems would add a meaty quality to veggie burgers and, yes, it worked! Now we find ourselves with too many portobello caps and not enough stems! We serve these veggie burgers on potato onion focaccia, accompanied with mashed potatoes or roasted rosemary potatoes, and sweet marinated onions (page 134).

1 zucchini, cut into ½-inch cubes
1 yellow squash, cut into ½-inch cubes
1 medium eggplant, cut into ½-inch cubes (unpeeled)
1 medium Spanish onion, diced
1 red bell pepper, chopped
2 whole portobello mushrooms or 6 portobello stems, chopped
1 cup chopped fresh spinach leaves
4 cloves garlic, minced
About ½ cup extra-virgin olive oil
1 cup rolled oats
¾ cup coarse cornmeal
½ cup dry bread crumbs
1 tablespoon or more hot sauce
½ teaspoon ground cumin
1 cup canned chickpeas, drained but liquid reserved
3 tablespoons olive oil
3 tablespoons fresh lemon juice
1½ cups whole-wheat flour
Salt and cracked pepper to taste
2 cups vegetable, peanut, or canola oil

1. Preheat the oven to 450 degrees.
2. Spread the zucchini, squash, eggplant, onion, pepper, mushrooms, spinach, and garlic on a baking sheet and drizzle with the extra-virgin olive oil. Roast the vegetables until they start to brown, 10 to 15 minutes. Let the roasted vegetables stand until they are cool enough to touch, then transfer to a large bowl.

3. Dry-roast the rolled oats on a baking sheet in the oven until golden brown, about 10 minutes. *Do not walk away—they burn easily!*
4. Add the oats, ¼ cup of the cornmeal, the bread crumbs, hot sauce, and cumin to the vegetables. Using your hands, combine everything well. Season with salt and pepper to taste.
5. Mash the chickpeas with the olive oil and lemon juice. Add this to the vegetable mixture and mix well. Using about ¼ cup of the mixture, shape 1 small patty as a test.
6. Combine the whole-wheat flour and remaining ½ cup cornmeal on a plate. Coat the test patty completely with the flour mixture.
7. Heat the oil in a deep skillet to 375 degrees. Add the test patty and deep-fry it until golden brown.
8. Taste the patty. If it seems too dry, add more mashed chickpeas with a little of their liquid. If it seems too wet, add more toasted oats and cornmeal.
9. Make any adjustments needed to the mixture and shape it into 6 to 8 burger-sized patties. Coat them completely with the flour mixture and fry 1 or 2 at a time until golden brown.
10. Serve immediately on your favorite bun or english muffin with anything you like on a burger.

Note: If you prefer, these veggie burgers can be pan-fried with only a little oil. I am not convinced, however, that pan-frying results in any less oil in the food. If the deep-frying oil is the right temperature, it does not seem that any more of it is absorbed than when pan-frying with ⅛ to ¼ inch oil in the pan. Using a nonstick pan and/or cooking spray, however, is another story.

4

STARTERS AND SMALL DISHES

*H*aving spent two years of my formative culinarily adolescence living in Spain, I took to the notion of little plates of food making a meal. Tapas bars (the name of the cafés serving these little tastes) were a regular part of life. What better way to eat a meal than to be able to sample a little of everything? Here, in the States, I have to settle for eating off other people's plates. Friends who eat out with me have come to learn that there is no such thing as keeping your own entrée.

As a caterer I often encourage people to skip the entrée and simply serve a wide selection of starters. If you want to have a really sexy cocktail party, allow guests to nibble all night, instead of sitting down to a big plate of food. Hot summer nights are perfect for snacking. One event in particular stands out as an example of a true tapas party. The house, with its grounds overlooking the Hudson, seemed cast for the set of *North by North West.* The party started at sunset. Carey and Heremes, the hosts, are natural entertainers. All evening, trays of different morsels were passed around. Curried crab salpicon quesadillas, pâté, sliced medallions of tenderloin with cilantro pumpkin-seed pesto, and much more. We gave the guests breathing time between new tastes. The curved black lacquered bar always had a plate on it of something delicate and yummy as well. Martini glasses could be heard tinkling through the night. The party stands out in my mind as a great success.

Remember, starters should never require a utensil.

Crudités and dip can be a fresh, colorful, nonfilling start to any meal. Of course, there are the traditional vegetable choices: carrots, celery, cucumbers, broccoli, cauliflower, radishes, bell peppers, and cherry tomatoes, but what about some more unusual vegetable choices like endive, fennel, or jícama?

Presentation is the key to crudités. Get three-dimensional: Instead of having vegetables all cut in uniform pieces, mix in whole, uncut fruits and vegetables to give both height and bold color.

Vegetables themselves make the best dip bowls. In the fall, I use an acorn squash for serving. Simply cut off the top with the stem and scoop out the seeds; cut a thin slice off the bottom, too, so the squash won't roll. You can use the outer leaves of a purple cabbage or hollow out a head of cabbage. Cut the tops off of bell peppers and fill them with dip. Cover the bottom of your platter with ruby chard leaves or red cabbage leaves. These simple tricks can make run-of-the-mill crudités into an exotic and dramatic presentation.

The spinach dip (page 118) and red pepper aioli (page 119) are colorful and fresh tasting. At Pongo these serve as our focal point and are often rounded out with a third, more traditional, dip, mushroom caps stuffed with mushroom boursin (page 136), or snow peas piped with a smooth cheese or crab dip.

SOME CRUDITÉS SUGGESTIONS:

Belgian endive leaves
Blanched fiddleheads
Sugar snap peas
Young, thin asparagus spears
Fennel
Jícama (peeled, sliced, then soaked in ice
  with lemon prior to serving)
Turnips
Snow peas
Whole fruits and vegetables for display
Bunches of red grapes
Large globe grapes
Tiny champagne grapes
Very small red or yellow sugar baby
  watermelons
Small seckel pears
Red pears
Tiny yellow, red, and green cherry
  tomatoes still on the vine

Whole yellow or heirloom striped or
  splotched tomatoes
Squash blossoms still attached to the
  green squash
Tomatillos with their husks still attached
  and pulled back
Small heads of radicchio

Note: Traditional dip starts with three parts sour cream to one part mayonnaise, then fresh herbs and seasoning are added. Just about everyone has made some variation of this dip. Seasonings include lemon, minced parsley, chives, dill, curry, paprika, Old Bay seasoning, Worcestershire sauce, horseradish, bacon, dried onion, minced dried shrimp, pesto. . . . Whatever floats your boat (as long as that boat is carved out of a vegetable and holds some dip).

Spinach Dip

This dip is a standard for crudités at Pongo. It tastes very fresh and clean.

2 tablespoons extra-virgin olive oil
1 cup Hellmann's mayonnaise
Salt and cracked pepper to taste
Juice of 1 lemon
1 pound fresh spinach, large stems
   removed, well washed and dried

1. Combine everything but the spinach in a blender or food processor until smooth.
2. With the machine running, feed in the spinach one handful at a time. It doesn't seem like it will all fit but, rest assured, it will.

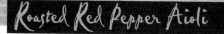
Roasted Red Pepper Aioli

Aioli is a French garlicky homemade mayonnaise, which starts simply with raw egg yolks and extra-virgin olive oil emulsified in a food processor or blender. If you have never made mayonnaise before, you should try it, for homemade is truly better than store-bought. As an alternative a good-quality store-bought mayonnaise, like Hellmann's, can be substituted. Once the other ingredients are added to it, the final product is quite acceptable. This aioli is recommended for serving with crudités (page 116), Sesame-Crusted Shrimp (page 130), and Scallion Corn Cakes (page 125), among other dishes.

HOMEMADE AIOLI:

2 large egg yolks
1 cup extra-virgin olive oil
4 cloves garlic, minced
Juice of 1/2 lemon
Salt and cracked pepper to taste
2 red bell peppers roasted and peeled
    (page 221)

1. Using an electric mixer or blender, beat the egg yolks until they are pale yellow. With the machine running, slowly drizzle in the olive oil. Add the garlic, lemon juice, salt, and pepper and mix until thoroughly combined.
2. Purée the roasted peppers separately and stir them into the aioli.

STORE-BOUGHT VERSION:

1 cup Hellmann's mayonnaise
2 tablespoons extra-virgin olive oil
4 cloves garlic, minced
Juice of 1/2 lemon
Salt and cracked pepper to taste
2 red bell peppers, roasted and peeled
    (page 221)

Combine all the ingredients in a blender or food processor.

Note: Dishes containing raw eggs carry the risk of salmonella, and should not be eaten by the very young, the very old, pregnant women or anyone with a compromised immune system.

This smoky, fresh, and spicy sauce is a variation of an old favorite.

One 28-ounce can fancy Italian plum
  tomatoes, drained
1 to 2 whole chipotles, dried or canned
  (if using dried, let the peppers sit
  in a splash of boiling water about
  20 minutes until soft)
2 tablespoons honey
1 cup loosely packed cilantro with stems,
  coarsely chopped, plus small sprigs for
  garnish
One 6-ounce can tomato paste
2 to 4 tablespoons horseradish, or more
  to taste
40 (4 per guest) cooked, peeled, and
  deveined medium-size shrimp (see Note)
Lemon wedges for garnish

1. Purée the tomatoes, chipotles, and honey in a blender or food processor.
2. Add the cilantro to the blender and quickly combine.
3. Pour the sauce into a bowl. Whisk in the tomato paste and horseradish.
4. Serve the sauce in a bowl surrounded by the shrimp. For a more dramatic presentation, spoon the sauce into martini glasses and arrange the shrimp with their tails hanging over the lip of the glass. Garnish with lemon wedges and cilantro sprigs. Serve with thin bread sticks or oyster crackers.

Note: To prepare the shrimp, first peel and devein them. Bring 2 quarts water to a boil in a large pan. Add 1 tablespoon salt and the shrimp. Boil just until the shrimp are evenly pink, 3 to 5 minutes. Do not overcook the shrimp. Immediately drain the shrimp and transfer to a large bowl of ice water to stop the cooking.

Candied-Pecan-Filled Pattypan Squash

This is very quick and easy to make. If you can find very small pattypans, you can serve them as a bite-sized hors d'oeuvre. If the pattypans are larger, serve them as a side dish with pork chops or ham. For the larger squash, adjust the other ingredients and allow an additional 10 to 15 minutes cooking time.

40 tiny or 24 medium pattypan squash
1 to 2 tablespoons olive oil
1 cup chopped pecans
2 tablespoons butter
Salt and cracked pepper to taste
2 tablespoons maple syrup
Dash of cayenne pepper (optional)

1. Preheat the oven to 375 degrees.
2. Using a sharp paring knife, hollow out the tops of the squash. They should look like deep little bowls. Cut a flat slice on the bottom removing any bumps, so they stand flat, but do not cut through the bottom of the squash.
3. Coat the squash with the olive oil and spread them out on a baking sheet. Bake until the squash are soft, about 15 minutes.
4. In a small sauté pan over medium heat, toast the pecans in the butter with salt and pepper. Add the maple syrup and cayenne, if using, to the pecans. Over medium heat, stir until the nuts are just starting to harden with the syrup. Spoon the nuts into the pattypans. Serve immediately.

At Pongo we plate these artichokes ahead of time and refrigerate them, then dress and garnish them when it's time to serve. The dressing tastes even better when made in advance. This is perfect for a sit-down summer dinner party. Serve with a cold pasta for dinner (like the soba noodles on page 152) and ginger crème brûlée. With everything prepared ahead of time, the only thing you'll have left to make is your martini.

4 fresh artichokes, trimmed
1 bay leaf
1 teaspoon coriander seeds
1 teaspoon whole peppercorns
1 whole garlic bulb, cut horizontally in half
2 tablespoons olive oil
1 tablespoon Dijon mustard
Juice of 2 lemons
1 cup aioli (page 119), made without the red peppers, or 1 cup good-quality mayonnaise mixed with 2 tablespoons olive oil
Salt and cracked pepper to taste
1 head red leaf or Bibb lettuce, leaves separated, washed, and dried
1 red bell pepper, roasted, peeled, and cut into strips (page 221) for garnish
Lemon wedges for garnish

1. Holding them by their stems, smash the artichokes on a flat surface to open the leaves a bit. Boil the artichokes in water to cover with the bay leaf, coriander, and peppercorns until the leaves pull off easily and the tips of the leaves are soft enough to scrape off with your teeth, about 45 minutes.

2. Cool the artichokes under cold running water, then chill them in the refrigerator. When they are cold, carefully cut them lengthwise in half. Using a teaspoon or grapefruit spoon, scoop out the soft little hairs on top of each artichoke heart.

3. In a little baking dish, drizzle the garlic with the olive oil. Roast in a 475-degree oven until it is golden brown, 20 to 25 minutes. Squeeze the garlic cloves out of their skins. Purée the garlic, mustard, and lemon juice until smooth, then mix in the aioli, salt, and pepper.

4. Plate the artichokes on lettuce leaves on 4 individual plates and dress with the aioli. Garnish with the red pepper strips and lemon wedges.

Note: For a brunch dish, serve these artichokes warm with hollandaise sauce (page 22).

Portobello Mushroom Caps with Herbed Goat Cheese and Balsamic Essence

This dish has a very elegant presentation. The broiled mushroom has an earthy meaty flavor that is complemented by the sharp zing of the balsamic essence. Serve one portobello cap per person with warm crusty bread to dip in the olive oil, which will become infused with the flavor of the mushroom and herbs.

This recipe makes enough herbed goat cheese for two mushrooms. You can triple the recipe and keep the extra in the fridge. Eat it on toast, in sandwiches, rolled into buttons for salads, as a cracker dip, and so on.

The balsamic essence keeps virtually forever, has many uses, and can be made way ahead of time. The vinegar is very pungent while it is reducing, so open a window and try to make it well before company arrives.

1 cup balsamic vinegar
1 tablespoon sugar
2½ ounces soft fresh goat cheese
2 teaspoons minced fresh herbs or pesto (any combination of basil, parsley, thyme, rosemary, or tarragon)

Salt and cracked pepper to taste
2 to 4 tablespoons extra-virgin olive oil
2 medium portobello mushrooms, cleaned and stems removed (see Note)
Small herb sprigs for garnish

1. In a small heavy saucepan, bring the vinegar and sugar to a boil. Reduce the heat to very low and simmer until the vinegar is reduced to half its volume. *Make sure the sauce does not burn.*

2. Combine the goat cheese with the herbs, salt, and pepper.

3. On a small baking sheet or shallow baking dish, pour the olive oil into the gills of the mushroom caps and on the bottom of the pan (enough so that the mushrooms can be served in a small pool of hot olive oil).

4. Roll the herbed goat cheese into 2 balls and use the balls to fill the circle where the mushroom stem was removed. Broil the mushroom cap until the goat cheese is golden brown and the oil is bubbling.

5. Pour the hot oil onto 2 plates. Slide a mushroom cap onto the center of each plate and drizzle some of the balsamic essence onto each plate. If you put the balsamic essence in a squeeze bottle, you can make designs on the plate and in the oil. Serve with cracked pepper and herb sprigs for garnish.

Note: Clean the mushroom caps with a damp paper towel or cloth; do not submerge them in water

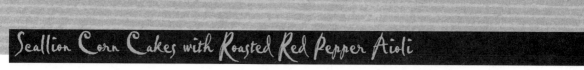

Scallion Corn Cakes with Roasted Red Pepper Aioli

These little savory pancakes are wonderful to make when corn is in season. They can be prepared ahead and reheated in the oven, but are best right out of the skillet.

> 2 cups Bisquick baking mix
> 1 large or 2 medium eggs
> ³/₄ cup milk
> 5 scallions, chopped, or 15 chives,
>   minced, plus several whole scallions or
>   chives for garnish
> 2 tablespoons minced parsley
> Dash of cayenne pepper
> Salt and cracked pepper to taste
> 4 or 5 ears fresh sweet corn, kernels cut
>   from the cobs
> 3 to 4 tablespoons butter
> Roasted Red Pepper Aioli (page 119) or
>   cilantro crème fraîche (page 131)

1. Whisk the Bisquick, egg, and milk together. Add the scallions, parsley, cayenne, salt, and pepper. Let stand for about 20 minutes, then fold in the corn.
2. In a heavy cast-iron skillet over medium heat, melt ½ tablespoon butter until bubbling. Drop about 1 tablespoon batter for each cake onto the skillet. Cook until golden brown on both sides. Repeat until the butter and batter are gone.
3. Garnish the cakes with whole chives (chive blossoms are nice, too). Serve with the red pepper aioli or cilantro crème fraîche as a dip.

SERVES 4 TO 6

Potato pancakes are among the most perfect foods known to mankind. There are almost as many variations of this very simple little cake as there are people who love them. Martha Stewart, and many others, recommend that the potatoes be soaked first to remove excess starch. Personally, I can't wait that long. This recipe is the simplest way to have great results. The pancakes must be made immediately after the potato is grated. If it sits, the potato will become gluey.

The pepper, lemon, and ginger added to the applesauce give it a real zing. If this sounds too out there, you can make traditional applesauce without them. If you're feeling particularly ritzy, skip the applesauce altogether and serve with a spoonful of sour cream and caviar on each pancake.

APPLESAUCE:

4 tart crisp apples, such as Granny Smith or Macoun, peeled, cored, and chopped
1 cup spring water
1 tablespoon maple syrup
1 tablespoon grated lemon zest
1 teaspoon cracked pepper
One 1/2-inch-thick piece fresh ginger, peeled and poked with a few holes so more flavor will be released

POTATO PANCAKES:

2 cups vegetable, peanut, or canola oil
2 large Idaho potatoes, peeled
1 small onion
3 tablespoons matzo meal
1 large egg

Sour cream for serving

FOR THE APPLESAUCE:

1. Simmer all the ingredients together in a saucepan over medium-low heat until the apples are soft, 15 to 20 minutes. Remove the ginger before serving.

FOR THE POTATO PANCAKES:

2. In a deep cast-iron skillet over medium heat, begin to warm the oil to 375 degrees. Do not allow it to smoke. On the large side of a box grater, grate the potatoes and onions into a bowl. Immediately add the matzo meal and egg to

the mixture. If you let the potato and onion sit around, they will become bitter and starchy.

3. Test the heat of the oil with a small dot of potato. If the potato does not bubble rapidly, the oil is too cold; if it bubbles and spatters furiously, the oil is too hot.

4. Drop (carefully!) a tablespoon of the potato mixture into the oil and flatten it with the back of the spoon; lacy edges of stray potato are great so don't worry about making them perfectly round. Fry just 4 pancakes at a time and don't fiddle with them until they have started to brown on one side—only flip them over. Fry them until they are evenly browned, drain on paper towels, and keep in a warm oven until all the pancakes are fried. Serve with the applesauce and sour cream.

I hate to burst any bubbles but "pâté" and chopped chicken liver are often the same thing. People often assume all pâté is pâté de foie gras, which is made with goose livers that have been inhumanely bloated to a quarter of the weight of the goose, but the word *pâté* basically implies ground liver. Chicken livers are very inexpensive, easy to find, and full of flavor. The difference between "pâté" and "chopped chicken liver" is the same as that between "Crispy Catfish" and "Deep-Fat-Fried Bottom Feeders."

1 pound chicken livers
4 tablespoons good-quality olive oil
5 shallots, minced
3 eggs, hard boiled and peeled
2 tablespoons Hellmann's mayonnaise
2 tablespoons sharp Dijon mustard
3 tablespoons finely minced baby dill
   pickles, preferably gherkins, or capers
1 tablespoon balsamic vinegar, or more to
   taste
Salt and cracked pepper to taste
Garlic Toasts (recipe follows)
Crushed pistachios and minced red onion
   for garnish

1. In a large heavy skillet over medium heat, sauté the livers in 2 tablespoons of the oil until slightly firm and no longer "bleeding." Do not overcook the livers. If you do, the texture will turn grainy instead of smooth and buttery. Check the livers by cutting one open.

2. Sauté the shallots in the remaining 2 tablespoons olive oil until translucent.

3. Place the hard-boiled eggs and livers in a food processor and process with pulses until smooth. Transfer the mixture to a bowl and stir in the shallots, mayonnaise, mustard, pickles, vinegar, salt, and pepper.

4. When you're ready to serve, spoon the pâté onto garlic toasts and garnish with crushed pistachios, minced red onion, and additional cracked pepper.

Garlic Toasts

1/3 cup extra-virgin olive oil
6 cloves garlic, minced
1/2 teaspoon salt
1 good-quality baguette (page 260), cut
   diagonally into 1/4-inch slices

1. Preheat the oven to 400 degrees.
2. In a very large bowl, combine the oil, garlic, and salt. Tilt the bowl to coat the sides with oil. Toss in the sliced bread and stir with your hands until the bread is coated with the oil.
3. Lay the bread in a single layer on baking sheets or large baking pans. Bake until golden brown, 13 to 15 minutes.

SERVES 4 TO 6

For almost every party I have ever catered, my clients request this dish. The hardest part is keeping kitchen helpers from eating too many of the shrimp. The bamboo skewers keep fingers clean but, more important, slow down the speed at which the shrimp are eaten. I usually serve this with peanut sauce, but roasted red pepper aioli (page 119) is very good as well. Allow the shrimp to marinate overnight.

> 2 pounds raw medium-size shrimp, peeled and deveined
> 1/2 cup toasted sesame oil
> 1 tablespoon grated lime zest
> 6 cloves garlic, minced
> 1 tablespoon minced fresh ginger
> Thin bamboo skewers, cut into 4-inch pieces
> 1 cup sesame seeds, toasted (see Note)
> Olive oil for sautéing the shrimp
> Thai Peanut Sauce (page 140)
> Thin lime wheels and small flat-leaf parsley or cilantro sprigs for garnish

1. The day before serving, toss the shrimp with the sesame oil, lime zest, garlic, and ginger. Let marinate overnight in the refrigerator.
2. Skewer the shrimp onto the bamboo sticks, piercing each one through the top and tail. Pour the sesame seeds out onto a plate or pie pan. In a large sauté pan over medium heat, sauté the shrimp in batches in olive oil until they are cooked all the way through. Immediately drop the hot shrimp in the sesame seeds and press the seeds onto the shrimp until they are completely coated. Let cool to room temperature.
3. Place the shrimp on a platter. Serve the peanut sauce in a bowl in the middle of the shrimp. Garnish with the lime wheels and herb sprigs.

Note: To toast sesame seeds, swirl them in a dry skillet over low heat until they are golden brown.

Shrimp and Hominy Cakes with Cilantro Crème Fraîche

These little cakes are crisp on the outside and soft and creamy on the inside. Both the grits cakes and the cilantro crème fraîche can be prepared ahead and the cakes simply broiled, grilled, or fried to order at the time of sewing. You can use the cilantro crème fraîche in many of the same ways you use sour cream: with quesadillas, nachos, as a dip for many of our starters, and so on. It also keeps a good long time.

SHRIMP AND HOMINY CAKES:
6 cups milk

7½ cups water

8 tablespoons (1 stick) butter

1 cup chopped scallions

½ cup fully cooked minced bacon (to taste)

2 cups grated Cheddar cheese (smoked Cheddar is really good if you can find it)

Salt and cracked pepper to taste

4 cups quick grits

1 pound shrimp, cooked, peeled, deveined, and chopped

Melted butter for cooking the cakes

CILANTRO CRÈME FRAÎCHE:
2 cups sour cream

Juice of 4 limes

3 tablespoons sliced pickled jalapeños with brine, or to taste

1 cup (loosely packed) cilantro sprigs, stems removed, plus several small sprigs for garnish

10 sprigs parsley, stems removed

1 cup (packed) spinach leaves

½ teaspoon ground cumin

1 teaspoon grated lime zest

FOR THE SHRIMP AND HOMINY CAKES:
1. In a heavy saucepan over medium heat, bring the milk and 6 cups of the water to a slow boil. Stir in the butter, scallions, bacon, Cheddar, salt, and pepper. Slowly whisk in the grits and reduce the heat to medium. Cook the grits until they no longer taste sandy or gritty, 5 to 7 minutes. Keep stirring from the bottom, for grits can stick. Stir in the remaining 1½ cups water just before

the grits finish cooking. The consistency you want is that of a thick porridge. Stir in the shrimp, divide the grits between 2 greased 15 × 10-inch baking sheets, and use a rubber spatula dipped in melted butter to smooth the top of the grits. Let cool to room temperature, then refrigerate them until they are fully chilled.

2. Cut the grits with a cookie cutter or the mouth of a white wineglass. These little cakes can be prepared a day ahead and kept cold. When you are ready to serve, brush the cakes with melted butter and broil or grill them on both sides on a greased baking sheet or cooking rack, until crisp and browned. Or they can be rolled in flour and deep-fried in 2 cups vegetable, peanut, or canola oil heated to 375 degrees.

FOR THE CILANTRO CRÈME FRAÎCHE:
3. Put the sour cream, lime juice, and jalapeños in a blender or food processor.
4. Coarsely chop the cilantro, parsley, and spinach. With the machine running, add the herb mixture to the blender. Stop and add the cumin and lime zest, then process until mixed.
5. Serve the little cakes hot with the cilantro crème fraîche. Garnish with cilantro sprigs.

SERVES 12

I have fond memories of making fondue at home as a kid. I think it is perfect fall and winter party fare. The flame looks cozy, the room fills with the smell of the simmering cheese, and, best of all, everyone has fun. It is the Swiss custom that when a lady loses her bread in the fondue she must kiss the nearest man; when a man loses his bread he must provide the next round of drinks. So dust off those old fondue pots or hit some yard sales and give a set a new home.

The presentation is very dramatic; we pile attractive whole loaves of bread around the fondue pots. For crunch and color, I also serve the fondue with raw veggies like mushrooms, broccoli, peppers, cauliflower, and cherry tomatoes.

2½ cups dry white wine	1 cup grated Cheddar cheese
4 cloves garlic, minced	1 cup grated Parmesan cheese
8 tablespoons (1 stick) butter	1 to 2 shots kirsch (cherry brandy)
½ cup all-purpose flour	Salt and white pepper to taste
4 cups milk, warmed	Assorted good-quality breads
1 cup grated Swiss, Jarlsberg, or Gruyère cheese	Assorted raw vegetables (optional)

1. In a small saucepan over medium-low heat, simmer the white wine with the garlic until the wine is reduced to half its volume.
2. At the same time, in a separate skillet over low heat, melt the butter. Add the flour, stir until smooth, and simmer for a few minutes, stirring frequently.
3. Scrape the flour mixture into the top of a double boiler set over about 2 inches of boiling water. Whisk in the warm milk, then slowly whisk in the cheeses. Stir in the reduced wine with the garlic, the kirsch, salt, and pepper. Serve warm in a fondue pot.
4. To serve, arrange baskets with whole loaves of bread. Have a cutting board and serrated knife on the table as well as a large plate of bread cut into 1-inch cubes. For large parties, I use bamboo skewers instead of fondue forks. It is an inviting presentation if you poke the skewers into the cut bread rather than simply keeping them on the side.

Note: For larger parties, use bamboo skewers instead of fondue forks.

Marinated onions are what distinguishes Cafe Pongo's quesadillas from the rest. A true onion lover will eat these onions like pickles right out of the jar. Every Pongo black Angus burger comes with a generous helping of these onions and mashed potatoes. People often ask for more onions. They also look really pretty in a Mason jar in the fridge. (For those of us who admire the interiors of our refrigerators.) Let the onions marinate overnight. I highly recommend serving the quesadillas with the cilantro crème fraîche (page 131) or traditonal salsa roja (page 23); salsa verde (page 37) and guacamole are great, too.

MARINATED ONIONS:

1/2 cup sugar
3 cups red wine vinegar
2 tablespoons fresh lemon juice
1 tablespoon whole coriander seeds, or 1 teaspoon ground coriander
1 teaspoon ground cumin
1/2 teaspoon ground allspice
1/4 cup chopped fresh cilantro leaves
1/2 cup olive oil
Salt and cracked pepper to taste
2 red onions, thinly sliced

QUESADILLAS:

6 good-quality flour tortillas, or 12 corn tortillas
3 to 4 cups sliced or grated Cheddar, Monterey Jack, or Oaxacan string cheese
Cilantro Crème Fraîche (page 131)

OTHER QUESADILLA FILLINGS

Shredded chicken
Fresh spinach leaves
Minced roasted poblano peppers
Sliced chorizo
Corn relish
Squash blossoms
Pickled jalapeños
My personal favorite: Oaxacan string cheese on blue corn tortillas with squash blossoms

FOR THE MARINATED ONIONS:

1. In a large mixing bowl, whisk the sugar in the vinegar until it is dissolved. Add all the remaining ingredients. Pour everything into a jar and let sit in the refrigerator at least overnight.

FOR THE QUESADILLAS:

2. Fold the flour tortillas in half with cheese and marinated onions in the middle. Corn tortillas are usually smaller, so place one on top of the other with the fillings in between. In a dry cast-iron skillet or comal over medium heat toast both sides until the cheese is completely melted. Cut the quesadillas into triangles. Serve hot with cilantro crème fraîche.

The mushroom-cheese mixture in this recipe, similar to the popular Boursin fla-vored cheeses, is very versatile. It can be stuffed into chicken breasts (page 190) or mushroom caps (shiitake, cremini, or white) or served with crackers. It can also be made ahead and refrigerated. The tarts themselves are best served warm out of the oven. A few mini-muffin tins are essential for making these petite hors d'oeuvres.

8 tablespoons (1 stick) unsalted butter
2 large shallots, minced
6 cloves garlic, minced
4 portobello mushroom caps with stems, wiped clean
12 medium-size white mushrooms, wiped clean
1 teaspoon fresh thyme leaves, or 1/2 teaspoon dried

Salt and cracked pepper to taste
8 ounces cream cheese
2 cups minced fresh flat-leaf parsley, plus additional leaves for garnish
1/2 cup dry bread crumbs
One 12-inch-square sheet frozen puff pastry, thawed in the refrigerator
1 egg beaten with 1 tablespoon water

1. In a medium skillet over medium heat, melt the butter. Add the shallots and garlic and sauté until translucent.

2. While the onions are cooking, purée the mushrooms in a food processor, or mince by hand. Add the mushrooms to the shallots along with the thyme, salt, and pepper. Cook until the mixture is dark and thick, 5 to 8 minutes.

3. Soften the cream cheese in the microwave for 3 minutes on low power. Place the cream cheese, parsley, and bread crumbs in a large bowl. Add the mush-room mixture and stir until combined and smooth.

4. Preheat the oven to 400 degrees.

5. Cut the puff pastry into 2-inch squares. (The squares can be rolled a little big-ger if they seem too small.) Grease 3 mini-muffin pans with cooking spray or butter. Lay the pastry squares over the muffin cups and gently push the pastry down into each cup, leaving the corners of the squares protruding from the cups. Using a teaspoon, carefully fill the pastry cups with the mushroom "Boursin." With a pastry brush, dab the egg wash over the tops of the tarts.

6. Bake the tartlets until puffed and golden brown; 15 to 20 minutes. Carefully loosen the tartlets from the muffin cups, garnish with parsley leaves, and serve hot.

Caramelized Onion Tart

This savory tart is best when made in a shallow tart pan with a removable bottom. Served room temperature, it is wonderful to have out on the kitchen table for guests to nibble on while sipping wine and keeping you company while you prepare dinner. It also makes a light lunch when accompanied by a salad.

THE ONIONS:

Basic Pie Dough (page 243)
4 huge Spanish onions, sliced ¼ inch
    thick
2 tablespoons olive oil

THE TART:

1 cup sour cream
2 large eggs
1 teaspoon fresh thyme leaves
4 ounces cream cheese, softened in the
    microwave

FOR THE ONIONS:

1. In a heavy cast-iron skillet, over low heat, slowly sauté the onion in the olive oil. Don't rush the process (it takes about 30 to 40 minutes) as the starch in the onions changes to sugar and the onions turn brown. This is referred to as caramelizing; there is *no* sugar added. When the onions are deep brown and taste sweet, they are done.

FOR THE TART:

2. Preheat the oven to 400 degrees.
3. Roll out the pie dough and press it into a 10-inch tart pan. Blind-bake the tart shell with pie weights on aluminum foil for 10 to 15 minutes. Remove and let cool. Reduce the oven heat to 350 degrees.
4. Transfer the onions to a mixing bowl and stir in the sour cream, eggs, and thyme. Stir in the cream cheese until thoroughly combined. Pour the onion mixture into the tart shell.
5. Bake the tart until set, about 20 minutes. Let it cool to room temperature before removing the rim of the pan and slicing.

These are served at Pongo with cilantro crème fraîche and pineapple chutney. The cilantro crème is very quick and easy to make. The chutney is a bit more involved, but you can make it ahead and keep it on hand. You can also substitute Ploughman's Apple Chutney (page 227) or a store-bought variety. The crème fraîche and chutney must be served with the samosas.

> 2 Idaho potatoes, peeled and cut into
>   large pieces
> 1 medium onion, diced
> 1 tablespoon olive oil
> 1/4 cup chopped scallions
> 1/4 cup chopped fresh cilantro, plus small
>   sprigs for garnish
> 1/2 teaspoon grated lemon zest
> 1 teaspoon curry powder
> 1/2 teaspoon ground cardamom
> 1/4 teaspoon ground cumin
> 1/4 cup fresh lemon juice
> 1/2 cup fresh or frozen peas
> Salt and pepper to taste
> Two 12-inch-square sheets frozen puff
>   pastry, thawed in the refrigerator
> 1 egg, beaten
> Cilantro Crème Fraîche (page 131)
> Pongo's Quick Pineapple Chutney (recipe
>   follows)

1. Preheat the oven to 400 degrees.
2. Boil the potato in water to cover until it is soft enough to mash. Drain.
3. In a sauté pan over medium heat, sauté the onion in the olive oil until it is translucent. Add the scallions, cilantro, lemon zest, curry powder, cardamom, and cumin; stir until the onion is evenly coated.
4. Scoop the onion mixture into a mixing bowl and deglaze the sauté pan with the lemon juice. Add the lemon juice to the mixing bowl. Add the potatoes and whip together. Fold in the peas. Add salt and pepper to taste.
5. On a floured surface, cut each sheet of puff pastry into nine 4-inch squares. (You can make them any size—bite size or individual large ones for each person.) Puff pastry sheets vary in size, so measure them to get perfect squares with as little waste as possible. Once you've cut the squares, put a scoop of potatoes on each one. Do not fill them so full that you can't pinch the edges closed. Using a pastry brush or the tips of your fingers, dab the egg

around the edges. Fold each square over to make a triangle. Crimp the edges closed with a fork. Brush or rub a little egg on top.

6. Bake on a nonstick baking sheet for 15 minutes. Turn the samosas over and brown the other side for 7 minutes. If you are making smaller samosas, they will cook faster. Garnish with the cilantro sprigs and serve immediately with the crème fraîche and chutney.

Pongo's Quick Pineapple Chutney

Chutney is actually quite simple. It's just some fruit and spices simmered with vinegar and sugar. Traditionally it is aged, but this chutney can be eaten immediately. Keep this chutney in the refrigerator; it lasts a very long time so you'll have lots of chances to explore your favorite ways to eat it. I love it with barbecued chicken.

1 ripe or overripe pineapple, peeled,
  cored, and chopped
4 tart apples, cored and chopped
  (do not peel)
2 red bell peppers, diced
2 tablespoons minced garlic
1/4 cup minced fresh ginger
2 whole lemons, cut in half
1 large Spanish onion, chopped
1 cup fresh lemon juice
3 cups cider vinegar
3 cups packed brown sugar
1 cup minced cilantro
1 tablespoon curry powder
1 tablespoon ground coriander
1 teaspoon ground cinnamon
1 teaspoon ground cardmom
1/2 to 1 teaspoon red pepper flakes
  (optional but necessary if you like
  spicy foods)

1. Combine all the ingredients in a large heavy saucepan, squeezing the juice from the lemon halves and dropping the lemon shells into the pan. Simmer over low heat for about hour. The chutney is done when all the liquid is absorbed into the fruit. Stir occasionally to prevent it from sticking on the bottom. Remove the lemon halves. May be stored in the refrigerator for up to 1 month.

SERVES 6

I could eat this peanut sauce with a spoon it is so good. This recipe will give you a good amount of sauce. It keeps well; we serve it with chicken satay, toss it with noodles for cold sesame noodles (rice vermicelli is best), and use it as a dip for sesame-crusted shrimp. The list goes on and on. One large chicken breast will make satay for two or three people.

THAI PEANUT SAUCE:

1 small to medium onion, minced
1 1/2 tablespoons minced garlic
3/4 cup olive oil
1 1/2 tablespoons red pepper flakes
Grated zest of 2 lemons
1 1/2 tablespoons minced lemongrass,
   preferably fresh
1 tablespoon curry powder
1 cup smooth or chunky peanut butter
1/2 cup packed brown sugar
1/4 cup fresh lemon juice
3 tablespoons Asian fish sauce
2 tablespoons sake
1 tablespoon rice wine vinegar
1/2 can coconut milk (7 ounces)

CHICKEN SATAY:

2 large whole skinless, boneless chicken
   breasts
Bamboo skewers, soaked in water for at
   least 30 minutes
2 tablespoons olive oil
2 teaspoons grated lemon zest
2 cloves garlic, minced

FOR THE PEANUT SAUCE:

1. In a heavy medium saucepan over medium heat, sauté the onion and garlic in the olive oil until the onion is translucent. Add the red pepper flakes, lemon zest, lemongrass, and curry powder; sauté for 1 minute.

2. Add all the remaining ingredients except the coconut milk. Simmer for 15 minutes. Remove from the heat and let cool almost to room temperature. Stir in the coconut milk. If you would like the sauce milder and can't imagine what to do with the rest of a can of coconut milk, add the remaining milk to taste.

FOR THE CHICKEN SATAY:

3. Trim the cartilage from between the halves of the chicken breast. Cut each half into 4 or 5 strips. Lay the strips flat and pound them to flatten them a little. Using the pointed end of the skewer, thread the stick through the chicken strips, piercing the meat 2 or 3 times. Marinate the chicken skewers in the olive oil, lemon zest, and garlic for at least 1 hour. Sauté or grill the chicken skewers until they are cooked all the way through. Serve with the peanut sauce for dipping.

So many home cooks are afraid of cooking duck, but a duck is basically a chicken that's all dark meat. I love dark meat. If you can cook a chicken, you can cook a duck. Take a few deep breaths. I'll walk you through it.

SLOW-COOKED DUCK:

1 whole duckling (most supermarkets carry them frozen), ready to cook, giblets removed
2 oranges, cut in half
¼ cup coarsely chopped fresh ginger
3 whole cloves garlic
2 tablespoons good-quality Chinese five-spice powder
6 bags Darjeeling tea
5 tablespoons soy sauce

VINAIGRETTE:

3 tablespoons hoisin sauce
2 tablespoons peanut butter
2 tablespoons rice wine vinegar
1 teaspoon Asian fish sauce
1 teaspoon hot chili oil
4 scallions, chopped

SPRING ROLLS:

5 to 7 ounces rice vermicelli or bean thread noodles
1 to 2 large heads red leaf, green leaf, or Bibb lettuce, leaves separated, washed and dried
4 sprigs mint, stems removed, plus additional leaves for garnish
2 cups bean sprouts
Chopped peanuts

FOR THE SLOW-COOKED DUCK:

1. In a stockpot, cover the duck with water. Add the oranges, ginger, garlic, five-spice powder, tea bags, and soy sauce. Simmer the duck uncovered over low heat until the broth has reduced in volume by about one-third.
2. Remove the duck from the stock and let it cool until it is cool enough to touch. Pick the meat off the bones and *save the skin.* Refrigerate the duck meat. Set aside ½ cup of the broth and discard the rest. (You can freeze the duck bones and at a later date make stock with them (see Basic Chicken Stock, page 67).

FOR THE VINAIGRETTE:

3. In a small bowl, mix all the ingredients for the vinaigrette together. Add a few tablespoons of the duck broth until it is the consistency of thick French dressing. Set aside.

FOR THE SPRING ROLLS:

4. Cook the noodles in a large pot of boiling water until they are al dente. Pour them into a strainer and cool under cold running water. Drain and set aside.
5. Cut the duck skins into ¼-inch strips. In a skillet, with a shake of salt on the bottom, over medium heat cook the duck skin until golden brown on both sides and completely crisp. These are cracklins.
6. To assemble the rolls, lay a few strips of duck meat in a lettuce leaf, then add a few cracklins, a large pinch of noodles, a mint leaf or two, some bean sprouts, a sprinkle of peanuts, and about 2 teaspoons of the hoisin vinaigrette. Be careful not to put so much in that you can't roll it closed. It's okay to leave the ends open. You may have to cut out the center seams of the lettuce for better rolling. Garnish the rolls with a few bean sprouts and mint leaves. Serve right away.

Note: If you use just a few strips of duck meat in each roll, you will have leftovers. The meat is so tasty, however, that you won't be sorry. Save it for a salad or toss it in a stir-fry.

5
ENTRÉES

*R*oland Butler has had a tremendous influence on the evolution of the dinner menu of Café Pongo. Roland and I attended college together, and in the summer of 1986, before Santa Fe expanded, Roland was the part-time brunch cook. He was in a band called Liquid Wrench; I had just started a restaurant. We would both end up working long into the night. At 6:00 A.M. sharp he would bang on my apartment door to get me up and with almost no sleep we would cook some great food. I still remember his juniper berry sausages. After graduation Roland moved to Philadelphia and became an accomplished chef. Then I heard that he wanted to move back to the Hudson Valley and was looking for a business interest. We got back in touch with each other and agreed to meet.

By the time he relocated, Roland and I had not seen each other in twelve years. He had achieved much in the intervening years, serving as *chef de cuisine* at the White Dog Café and The Striped Bass in Philadelphia. Once Roland joined the Pongo staff, I knew I was in the presence of true genius.

SERVES 1 (TWICE)

This little recipe is for lazy days; none of the ingredients need be fresh. This is a perfect meal for enjoying alone in front of the television, perhaps watching yet another episode of *Friends*. Do you ever wonder why you are unable to have more than one friend who shares the same height, weight, demographic, and hairstyle as you? How do they afford those Manhattan apartments?

Stay in your pajamas. Let all worries slip from your mind, as you twirl the strands of pasta in this tangy sauce.

2 tablespoons butter
1 tablespoon olive oil
4 cloves garlic, minced
1 large yellow onion, chopped
One 28-ounce can whole tomatoes,
   drained and chopped
1 teaspoon sugar
2 teaspoons whole fennel seeds
Salt and cracked pepper to taste
20 Kalamata or dry-cured Moroccan
   olives, pitted
2 to 4 anchovies, mashed
2 cups dry red wine
3 to 4 ounces linguine, or whatever pasta
   you have around, cooked al dente

1. In a large, heavy sauté pan over medium heat, melt 1 tablespoon of the butter in the olive oil. Add the garlic and onion and cook, stirring, until the onion is translucent.

2. Add the tomatoes and cook, stirring, until the tomatoes are rapidly bubbling. Stir in the sugar, fennel seeds, salt, and pepper. Reduce the heat and simmer for about 15 minutes, stirring occasionally. Add the olives, anchovies, and wine. Increase the heat to medium-high and cook, stirring constantly, for another 5 minutes to cook off the alcohol in the wine. Reduce the heat, taste for seasoning, and, for good measure, swirl in the remaining tablespoon of butter. Ladle over a bowl of piping hot linguine.

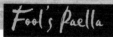

Fool's Paella

This recipe is virtually foolproof, unlike its rice counterpart. Leftover fully cooked chicken, shrimp, scallops, pork, chorizo, or any combination thereof can also be thrown in with the stock before adding the couscous.

4 cloves garlic, minced
1 medium onion, halved lengthwise, then
    cut crosswise into half-moon slices
1 red bell pepper, chopped
3 cups quartered cremini or white
    mushrooms (10 ounces)
2 tablespoons olive oil
1 cup frozen peas
Two 0.1-gram packets Zafferano (fake
    saffron), or 1 pinch saffron threads
1 to 2 pickled hot cherry peppers,
    stemmed, seeded, and chopped
2 cups chicken or vegetable stock
    (page 67 or 65)
2 tablespoons balsamic vinegar
Salt and cracked pepper to taste
One 10-ounce box couscous

1. In a sauté pan over medium heat, sauté the garlic, onion, bell pepper, and mushrooms in the olive oil until tender, about 10 minutes.
2. Add the remaining ingredients except the couscous and bring to a boil. Stir in the couscous, cover the pan, remove from the heat, and let stand 5 minutes. Serve immediately.

When I owned the Santa Fe restaurant, we would convert our refried black beans into this entrée by adding vegetables and salsa to the beans and broiling cheese over the top. A favorite dish of a certain former Simon and Schuster executive and friend without whom this book would not exist, this is a great way to use leftover black beans.

The *leftover* leftover Santa Fe black beans and extra sautéed zucchini are really good in an omelet, with salsa and sour cream on top.

> 1 zucchini, chopped
> 1 red bell pepper, chopped
> 1 tablespoon olive oil
> 4 cups Santa Fe Black Beans (page 216) or
>   good-quality canned black beans,
>   drained and rinsed
> 1 cup good-quality chunky salsa, home-
>   made or store-bought
> 1/4 cup chopped fresh cilantro
> 2 cups grated Monterey Jack or Cheddar
>   cheese
> 4 to 6 ounces sour cream (optional)
> Ornamental purple cabbage leaves,
>   minced red bell pepper, and cilantro
>   sprigs for garnish

1. In a medium saucepan over medium heat, sauté the zucchini and bell pepper in the oil until tender.
2. Add the black beans, salsa, and cilantro and simmer for 20 minutes.
3. Ladle the mixture into 4 individual ovenproof bowls, place the bowls on a baking sheet, and sprinkle the grated cheese on top. Broil until the cheese is golden brown. If you're feeling particularly sporty, you can do as they do in restaurants when browning French onion soup or crème brûlée and melt the cheese with your handy blowtorch (no kitchen should be without). A self-lighting trigger model is preferable. Just torch away until the top is golden brown. No goggles necessary.
4. Using oven mitts, lift the bowls onto dinner plates. Lay a small ornamental cabbage leaf on top of each bowl and scoop some sour cream, if using, into the cabbage cups. Sprinkle with minced red pepper and cilantro sprigs for crunch and color. Serve immediately.

SERVES 4

This is the single most popular dish I have ever put on a menu. It can be served either hot or cold. The pasta is sautéed in clarified butter until golden brown and crispy, and is then tossed with the greens, lemon juice, pine nuts, red pepper flakes, and feta. The cheese is tossed in the pan so it softens and melts a bit. This is a delicious vegetarian dish, but pan-seared shrimp are an elegant addition.

PASTA:

1 pound penne pasta
2 to 3 tablespoons olive oil
2 to 4 tablespoons clarified butter
  (see Note)
Salt and cracked pepper to taste (not too
  much salt, because the feta is salty)
8 shallots, minced

GREENS:

4 cups (packed) stemmed and torn kale
  leaves
1/2 head Savoy or green cabbage, cored
  and sliced
1 to 2 tablespoons good-quality olive oil
8 cloves garlic, minced
1 cup crumbled good-quality feta cheese,
  plus additional for garnish
3 tablespoons coarsely chopped fresh
  basil
3 tablespoons coarsely chopped fresh
  flat-leaf parsley
1 pound spinach, stems removed, washed,
  and dried

2 lemons, cut into wedges
1/4 cup pine nuts, toasted
Red pepper flakes
3 to 6 peeled and deveined shrimp per
  person, browned in olive oil (optional)

FOR THE PASTA:

1. Bring a large pot of water to a rolling boil. Add the penne and cook until it is *edible* but still quite firm. Drain the pasta in a colander. Immediately pour the olive oil over the penne and toss so that the pasta does not stick together. Cool under cold running water to completely stop the cooking. (The pasta will be cooked again, so at this stage it must be left underdone.)

2. In a large sauté pan over medium heat, pour in some of the clarified butter; don't allow the butter to turn brown or smoke. Drop in some penne and add a little salt and pepper. Shake the pan around until at least one side of the penne is golden brown. If you go too far, the pasta will either burn or become hard and dried out. When the pasta is almost done, add some shallots. Let them cook the rest of the way with the penne. Depending on the size of your pan, this process may have to be repeated a few times until all the penne and shallots have been seared.

FOR THE GREENS:

3. In another large sauté pan over high heat, sauté the kale and cabbage in the olive oil until soft and slightly browned but not mushy. Add the garlic and sauté for another minute or two. Add the feta, basil, and parsley. Toss the greens with the penne and, lastly, toss in the spinach. The spinach only needs to be wilted.

4. Divide the penne and greens among 4 plates. Squeeze a lemon wedge over each plate. Crumble more feta on top and sprinkle with pine nuts and red pepper flakes. Place the shrimp, if using, and lemon wedges on the very top of each dish.

Note: To make clarified butter, simply melt 3 to 5 tablespoons butter. Let stand. When the butter has separated, pour the "oil" off the top. This is clarified butter. Discard the cloudy, milky part at the bottom.

SERVES 4

Mustard greens are sadly underutilized. In this dish, their sharp, zesty flavor is mellowed by the sweet buckwheat flavor of the soba noodles. This is my brother Nick's recipe. I have never made it for the restaurant; it has always been reserved for family.

> 6 tablespoons sunflower seeds
> 3 tablespoons safflower or corn oil
> 1 large leek
> One 16-ounce package soba noodles
> 2 tablespoons dark miso paste
> 1 cup vegetable stock (page 65), or
>   1 bouillon cube dissolved in 1 cup water
> 4 cups (packed) coarsely chopped collard
>   greens, large stems removed, washed
>   and dried
> 4 cups (packed) chopped mustard greens,
>   washed and dried
> 4 cups (packed) chopped kale, washed
>   and dried
> 6 cloves garlic, minced
> ¼ teaspoon red pepper flakes
> 1 lemon, sliced into thin wheels

1. Start a pot of water boiling for the pasta.
2. In a small skillet over medium heat, toast the sunflower seeds in 1 tablespoon of the oil until golden brown. Remove from the heat and set aside.
3. Remove the tough outermost leaves of the leek. Cut all of the leek (white and green) into ¼-inch slices. Submerge the pieces in a bowl of cold water, deep enough so that the dirt on the leeks can drop to the bottom of the bowl without settling back on the leek. Fan out the leeks in the water, making sure all the stubborn grit has been removed. Lift the clean leek slices from the top of the water and pat dry.
4. In a wok or large skillet, over medium-high heat, sauté the leek in the remaining 2 tablespoons oil until tender and slightly browned.
5. When the pasta water reaches a rolling boil, drop in the soba noodles. Cook for exactly 2 minutes or follow package directions. When the soba is cooked, immediately pour it into a colander and cool completely under cold running water.
6. Dissolve the miso paste in the stock. Add the collard greens to the leek. Stir

the leek slices to the top to prevent burning. Cook the collards until they begin to become tender. Add the remaining greens, the miso mixture, garlic, and pepper flakes. Cook, stirring, until tender. Toss in the soba noodles and mix them with the greens until they are heated through. Pour into a warmed serving bowl. Finally add the toasted sunflower seeds, and toss them with the greens and noodles. Serve immediately, garnished with the lemon wheels.

Angel Hair Pasta with Parsley Almond Pesto, Roasted Red Peppers, Olives, and Artichokes

For me there can never be too many olives or artichokes, thus the birth of this dish. At Pongo, and at home, I always have a few different pestos on hand in the freezer. Extra pesto can be frozen in ice-cube trays, then cracked into a freezer bag and used later. (This is an old Martha Stewart trick.) This pesto has two variations, each completely different but equally delicious. Made with raw garlic and almonds, parsley pesto can be used in the same ways as basil pesto. Toasting the almonds and garlic together (see page 155), however, changes the flavor and mood of the pesto. Without toasting, the pesto tastes very fresh and clean. When the nuts are toasted, the pesto has a wintery, nutty flavor. The roasted red pepper and artichokes are versatile; they do both summer and winter.

PESTO:

1 large bunch flat-leaf parsley, stems trimmed
1 cup good-quality olive oil
1/2 cup sliced blanched almonds
6 cloves garlic, peeled
1 teaspoon grated lemon zest
2 to 4 tablespoons fresh lemon juice
Salt and cracked pepper to taste
1/2 cup grated Parmesan cheese

1 cup roasted and peeled red bell peppers (page 221) cut into strips
1 cup artichoke hearts marinated in oil
1/2 cup pitted Kalamata olives
2 tablespoons good-quality olive oil
1 pound angel hair pasta
Shaved Romano or Parmesan cheese for garnish
Cracked pepper to taste

FOR THE PESTO:

1. Set aside a few small sprigs of parsley for garnish. Fill a food processor or blender with about two-thirds of the remaining parsley. Add a little oil and purée. With the machine running, slowly add the almonds, garlic, lemon zest, lemon juice to taste, salt, and pepper. Feed in the remaining parsley with the Parmesan cheese and the remaining oil.

2. Bring a large pot of water to a rolling boil for the pasta.

3. In a medium skillet over medium heat, heat the roasted red pepper strips, artichokes, and olives in 1 tablespoon of the olive oil.
4. Add the pasta to the boiling water and cook until tender but still firm to the bite. Drain the pasta in a colander. Immediately pour the remaining 1 table-spoon olive oil over the pasta and toss so that the noodles do not stick to-gether.
5. In a large serving bowl, toss the piping-hot pasta with the pesto. Slide the hot artichokes, olives, and peppers on top. Garnish with shaved cheese, cracked pepper, and the remaining sprigs of parsley.

Toasted Almond and Garlic Pesto

If you would like to toast the almonds and garlic, cover them with some of the olive oil in a small skillet. Swirl them over medium heat until they are golden brown. For the toasted almond and garlic pesto, follow the same pesto directions but add 2 tablespoons more lemon juice.

SERVES 6

The roasted carrots, caramelized onions, and fresh spinach give this version of an old favorite new flavor, color, and texture. The pasta and vegetables are baked in the creamy béchamel with a deep, golden brown crust of crispy Cheddar and Brie broiled on top.

CARROTS:

> 2 pounds carrots
> 1 to 2 tablespoons good-quality olive oil
> 2 tablespoons dried basil

BÉCHAMEL:

> 8 tablespoons (1 stick) butter
> 1/2 cup all-purpose flour
> 4 cups milk, warmed
> 1/2 cup grated or diced Cheddar cheese
> 1/2 cup grated or diced Swiss cheese
> 1/2 cup grated or diced Parmesan cheese
> 2 tablespoons fresh thyme leaves

PASTA:

> 1 pound penne pasta
> 1 to 2 tablespoons olive oil

TO FINISH THE DISH:

> 1 pound fresh spinach, large stems
>   removed, washed, and dried
> 1/4 cup Caramelized Onions (page 137)
> 2 to 3 cups grated or sliced good-quality
>   Cheddar cheese
> 12 thin slices Brie
> Parsley sprigs, for garnish

FOR THE CARROTS:

1. Preheat the oven to 400 degrees.
2. Peel the carrots, then cut diagonally into ½-inch-thick pieces. Spread them out on a baking sheet and sprinkle with the olive oil and basil. Roast the carrots, stirring occasionally, until *browned,* about 10 to 15 minutes, or according to taste. (These carrots are great as a side dish by themselves!) Remove the carrots from the oven and reduce the oven heat to 350 degrees.

FOR THE BÉCHAMEL:

3. In a medium-size heavy saucepan over low to medium heat melt the butter. Whisk in the flour and let bubble for 3 to 4 minutes, stirring frequently. Whisk in the warm milk, then whisk in the cheeses and thyme. Continue to whisk over low heat until smooth and thickened. (The béchamel will keep in the refrigerator for over a week if well covered; it's great in lasagna.)

FOR THE PASTA:

4. Bring a large pot of water to a rolling boil. Add the penne, stir, and cook until the pasta is beginning to soften but is still quite firm. Pour the pasta into the colander and immediately toss with the olive oil to prevent it from sticking together. Cool the pasta under cold running water to completely stop the cooking. (It will be cooked again, so at this stage it must be left underdone.)

TO FINISH THE DISH:

5. Press the fresh spinach leaves in the bottom of a 2-inch-deep casserole or 4 individual baking dishes. Top the spinach with the caramelized onions, then layer the carrots and penne over the onions. Spoon in the béchamel until the dish is full. Cover the top with the Cheddar.
6. Bake until the casserole is heated all the way through, 15 to 20 minutes. Remove the dish from the oven and arrange the Brie slices on top. Increase the oven heat to 425 degrees. When the temperature is reached, return the dish to the oven and bake until the top is golden brown. Garnish with parsley sprigs.

Curried Lentil and Pear Harvest Purses with Lemon Yogurt Sauce

YIELDS ONE DOZEN PURSES; SERVES 4 TO 6

These are a fall treat. I serve them on individual plates, surrounded by a tangy watercress salad with blood orange vinaigrette. The "purses" can be assembled in the muffin tin, wrapped and frozen, then baked when needed.

LENTILS:

8 ounces brown lentils
1 medium onion, diced
4 cloves garlic, minced
2 tablespoons olive oil
2 tablespoons butter
2 tablespoons curry powder
1/2 cup golden raisins
3/4 cup chopped walnuts
1/2 cup apple cider
2 ripe red pears, cored and diced (unpeeled)
Salt and cracked pepper to taste

PURSES:

One 12-inch-square sheet frozen puff pastry, thawed in the refrigerator
1 egg lightly beaten with a splash of cold water

LEMON YOGURT SAUCE:

2 cups good-quality plain yogurt, such as Stonyfield (do not use low- or nonfat yogurt or yogurt with added gelatin or thickeners)
6 tablespoons fresh lemon juice
1 teaspoon grated lemon zest
Salt and cracked pepper to taste

FOR THE LENTILS:

1. Rinse the lentils and check for stones. Place the lentils in a small pan and add enough water to cover by 1/2 inch. Boil until tender, about 30 minutes.
2. In a heavy saucepan over medium heat, sauté the onion and garlic in the olive oil and butter until golden brown. Add the curry powder, raisins, and nuts. Hold the pan just above the flame and either lightly shake it or stir until the nuts are golden brown, the raisins are plump, and the curry is fragrant. Add half the cider, all the pears, salt, and pepper; cook until the pears are tender. Remove from the heat.

3. When the lentils are cooked, drain them and add them to the pear mixture. Combine well and add the remaining cider if the lentils begin to stick to the bottom of the pan.

FOR THE PURSES:

4. Preheat the oven to 350 degrees.
5. Place the sheet of puff pastry on a floured surface and roll a rolling pin over it a couple of times to make it even and slightly thinner. Cut into twelve 4 × 3-inch rectangles.
6. Grease a 12-cup muffin tin. Place 1 square of pastry in each cup. Divide the lentil filling among the cups. Dab a little egg wash on the corners of each pastry and pinch together the points of the dough into a cinched purse. Brush the tops with egg wash. Place in the oven and bake until puffed and golden brown, about 20 minutes.

FOR THE LEMON YOGURT SAUCE:

7. While the purses are baking, combine the yogurt, lemon juice, lemon zest, salt, and pepper.
8. Serve the purses immediately with the yogurt sauce on the side.

Vegetable Fritters with Green Curry Sauce and Ginger-Infused Basmati Rice

This dish is a vegan's dream. The green curry sauce is savory and creamy, while the rice adds a hint of sweetness. The crunch of the toasted coconut contributes a pleasant textural contrast. I recommend serving this with blanched kale, which carries the sauce well. The fritter mix will keep refrigerated for a few days but does not freeze well. The end result is well worth the fuss, and if all the fritters are not devoured, save the mix for veggie burgers a day or two later.

RICE:

1 medium onion, minced
2 tablespoons minced fresh ginger
2 tablespoons olive oil
2 cups basmati rice
2½ cups spring water
Half a 13.5-ounce can coconut milk (remaining half will be stirred into the curry)

CURRY SAUCE:

Half a 13.5-ounce can coconut milk
1½ cups finely minced fresh herbs, such as basil, cilantro, and parsley
4 teaspoons brown sugar
½ unsalted vegetable bouillon cube
1½ teaspoons Asian fish sauce or soy sauce
1 teaspoon green curry paste (available at health food stores and Asian markets)
1 teaspoon curry powder

FRITTERS:

Roasted Vegetable and Chickpea Burger mixture (page 112), shaped into 2-inch-wide fritters
Whole-wheat flour for coating
2 cups vegetable, peanut, or canola oil

Blanched kale or other greens of your choice for serving
½ cup toasted coconut (page 54) for garnish
Minced red bell pepper for garnish

FOR THE RICE:

1. In a medium saucepan over low heat, sauté the onion and ginger in the olive oil until the onion is translucent. Do not brown. Add the rice and stir until the rice is evenly glazed. Pour in the water. Cover and simmer over very low heat until all the water is absorbed, 20 to 25 minutes. Fluff the rice with a fork while adding the coconut milk. (Note that even off the heat, the rice will continue to cook, which will make it mushy if not served immediately. I recommend scooping the hot rice into a shallow pan to cool, and reheating it in a microwave when ready to serve.) Serve immediately.

FOR THE CURRY SAUCE:

2. Combine all the ingredients in a heavy saucepan. Bring to a boil, reduce the heat, and simmer until the liquid is reduced in volume by about a third.

FOR THE FRITTERS:

3. Coat the veggie patties in flour and fry in the oil heated to 375 degrees until golden brown on both sides. Repeat in batches until all the fritters are fried. Drain on paper towels.

4. To serve, place a scoop of rice in the center of each of 4 plates. Arrange a circle of blanched kale around the rice. Place the fritters on the greens and ladle the green curry sauce over the greens and fritters. Garnish with the toasted coconut and minced red pepper.

SERVES 6

Risotto is the archetype of Old World comfort food. This risotto is a very social dish because it requires constant attention and draws people into the kitchen with the strong, woody smell of the simmering rosemary and mushrooms. This recipe, given to me by my friend Yan, calls for two to three cups red wine; the remains of the bottle ought to be finished before the risotto is done. Have a second bottle ready to serve with the meal. The risotto can be served scooped over a broiled mushroom cap, garnished with sprigs of fresh rosemary, and with an arugula salad. The essence is a syrup made with balsamic vinegar. It keeps forever, has many uses, and can be made far in advance. The vinegar is very pungent while it is reducing, so open a window and try to have it finished before company arrives.

BALSAMIC ESSENCE:

1 cup balsamic vinegar
1 tablespoon sugar

STOCK:

6 cups chicken stock (page 67)
3 cloves garlic, smashed
4 or 5 sprigs rosemary
Salt and cracked pepper to taste
6 portobello mushroom stems

MUSHROOM CAPS:

6 portobello mushroom caps (save the
   stems for the stock)
2 tablespoons olive oil

RISOTTO:

2/3 cup chopped dried porcini mushrooms
1 large Spanish onion, minced
1/4 cup olive oil
2 tablespoons butter
3 cloves garlic, minced
1 pound Arborio rice
2 to 3 cups dry red wine
3 heaping tablespoons mascarpone
   cheese, plus additional for garnish
Salt and cracked pepper to taste

Arugula, watercress, frisée, or mesclun
   lettuce mix (optional)
Rosemary sprigs, extra-virgin olive oil,
   and cracked pepper for garnish

For the balsamic essence:

1. In a small heavy saucepan, bring the vinegar and sugar to a boil. Reduce the heat to very low and simmer until the vinegar is reduced by at least half its volume and is as thick as syrup in consistency. *Do not burn!* The essence can be put in a plastic squeeze bottle to make for a more professional presentation at the end.

For the stock:

2. In a soup pot, bring the chicken stock, garlic, rosemary, salt, and pepper to a rapid boil. Add the mushroom stems and reduce the heat, keeping the stock just below a boil.

For the mushroom caps:

3. Drizzle the mushroom caps with the olive oil and broil them until the oil bubbles.

For the risotto:

4. Pour boiling water over the dried porcini and let soak for 2 to 3 minutes. Remove the mushrooms from the water and set aside. Add the soaking water to the stock that is heating on the stove.

5. In a large heavy saucepan over low heat, sauté the onion in the olive oil and butter until translucent. Add the garlic and cook until the garlic is also translucent. Add the rice and stir until the rice is translucent from absorbing the moisture in the pot. Add 1 cup of the stock. Throughout the cooking process, which takes about 30 to 35 minutes, the rice should be regularly stirred and kept as moist as possible for best results. Add more stock, 1 cup at a time, as it is absorbed. (Now is the time to offer your friends another glass of wine, since they thought dinner was nearly ready when they arrived.)

6. Once the rice begins to swell, start adding the red wine instead of the stock. When the risotto is about ready, add the porcini mushrooms. Taste the risotto as you go. When the risotto is still al dente but not too crunchy, it is done. Stir in the mascarpone and season with salt and pepper to taste. Make sure the risotto is very moist, almost watery, when finished, because the rice will continue to absorb liquid. *Do not overcook!* Stir, cover, and let stand for a couple of minutes, which will allow it to thicken enough to hold its shape.

To finish the dish:

7. Arrange some of the greens, if using, on each of 6 individual plates as a bed for the mushroom cap. Place a packed teacup full of risotto in each broiled mushroom cap. (Reheat the caps if they have cooled down.) Garnish each serving with a small dollop of mascarpone and a sprig of fresh rosemary. Drizzle with extra-virgin olive oil and top with some cracked black pepper. Drizzle or squeeze from the bottle the balsamic essence in patterns on the plate. Serve immediately.

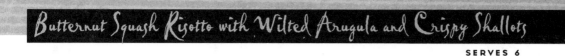

Butternut Squash Risotto with Wilted Arugula and Crispy Shallots

As flavorful as risotto is, I find it difficult to eat a whole bowl for dinner, as the texture can be slightly monotonous. The crunch of the arugula and the crispy shallots in the dish complement the smooth texture of the risotto. In the winter, we serve this with oven-roasted shoestring parsnips (page 210). I highly recommend their inclusion.

As most of my family is vegetarian, this dish was served as the main course for our Christmas dinner, 1999.

SQUASH:

>2 medium butternut squash, peeled, seeded, and cut into 1-inch cubes
>2 tablespoons olive oil

SHALLOTS:

>6 shallots, thinly sliced
>1 cup vegetable, peanut, or canola oil

RISOTTO:

>1 large Spanish onion, minced
>2 tablespoons olive oil
>2 tablespoons butter
>1 pound Arborio rice
>6 cups vegetable stock, (page 65), heated
>1 cup dry white wine
>3 bunches arugula, large stems removed, washed, and dried
>Shoestring Parsnips (page 210)

FOR THE SQUASH:

1. Preheat the oven to 375 degrees.
2. Coat the butternut squash with the olive oil and spread on a baking sheet. Roast, stirring occasionally, until softened, about 20 minutes.

FOR THE SHALLOTS:

3. In a small heavy saucepan over medium heat fry the shallots in the oil until they are golden brown. Spread them out on a paper towel and let them dry in a warm spot, like the top of a toaster oven on its lowest setting. This will prevent them from becoming soggy.

For the risotto:

4. In a large heavy saucepan over medium heat sauté the onion in the oil and butter until translucent.

5. Add the rice and the roasted squash and begin stirring constantly over low heat. Add the vegetable stock 1 cup at a time; do not add the next cup until the first has been absorbed. Midway through this process substitute the wine for the stock. Taste the risotto as you go. Cook the risotto until it is still al dente—firm but not crunchy. It will take 30 to 35 minutes. *Do not overcook it!* Make sure the risotto is very moist, almost watery, when finished, because the rice continues to absorb liquid. Stir, cover, and let stand for a few minutes. If you let the rice sit in the pot too long, the risotto will continue to cook from its own heat. So when it reaches the perfect consistency, serve it *immediately.*

To finish the dish:

6. Divide the arugula among 6 serving plates, laying the leaves flat. Scoop the risotto onto the center of each plate; the greens will wilt from its heat. Sprinkle the shallots over the risotto. Garnish the center of each dish with a generous haystack of the parsnips.

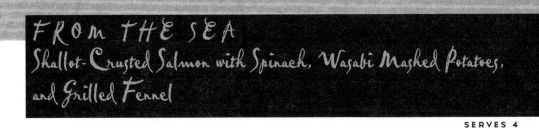

SERVES 4

The salmon fillets can be prepared immediately, but they will be easier to work with if they have been tightly wrapped in plastic wrap and refrigerated for a couple of hours after they have been crusted. They will even keep well overnight or can be frozen until needed.

SALMON:

1¼ cups all-purpose flour
¼ cup cornmeal
¾ cup plain dry bread crumbs
½ cup Rice Krispies cereal (yes, you read right!)
8 shallots, minced
2 large eggs
1 cup milk
Salt and cracked pepper to taste
Four 6-ounce salmon fillets
2 cups vegetable, peanut, or canola oil

MASHED POTATOES:

5 Idaho potatoes (see Note)
3 cups milk, warmed
3 shallots, finely diced
8 tablespoons (1 stick) butter, chilled, cut into 1-inch pieces
1 tablespoon wasabi powder
2 teaspoons horseradish

FENNEL:

1 to 2 bulbs fresh fennel, cut lengthwise into ½-inch-thick slices
1 to 2 tablespoons olive oil

SPINACH:

1 pound fresh spinach, stems removed, washed, and dried
4 cloves garlic, minced
1 to 2 tablespoons olive oil

Toasted sesame seeds (page 130) and additional wasabi powder mixed with water and shaped into small balls or cones can be served for added heat to those who desire it

For the salmon:

1. In a shallow pan or bowl, combine ¼ cup of the flour, the cornmeal, bread crumbs, Rice Krispies, and shallots. (If the shallots are minced in a food processor, do not purée them. If they are wet and stick together, they will be bitter and turn the salmon crust soggy.) With clean, dry hands, mix the ingredients together, crunching the Rice Krispies a little.
2. In a separate bowl, beat the eggs and milk together lightly.
3. Mix the remaining 1 cup flour with a dash each of salt and pepper on a plate.
4. Roll 1 salmon fillet in the seasoned flour, dip it in the egg mixture, then coat with the shallot mixture. With clean, dry hands, press the shallot mixture onto the fish so that it completely coats it. If you want the breading to be thicker, drizzle a little of the egg mixture with a teaspoon over the top of the salmon and coat it again. Repeat with the remaining fillets one at a time.
5. Tightly wrap the salmon individually in plastic wrap and refrigerate until just before cooking.

For the potatoes:

6. Peel, chop, and rinse the potatoes. Boil in water to cover until soft. Drain in a colander but do not allow the potatoes to cool. Allowing the potatoes to cool before whipping or overwhipping will make gluey mashed potatoes. Transfer the hot potatoes to a mixing bowl.
7. When the potatoes are almost done, bring the milk and shallots to a simmer in a small heavy saucepan.
8. Using a mixer, combine the milk mixture, the cold butter, the wasabi, and horseradish with the potatoes and whip until smooth. The potatoes taste best when they are eaten soon after they are mashed.

For the fennel:

9. While the potatoes are boiling, in a heavy skillet over low to medium heat, slowly brown both sides of the fennel slices in the olive oil.

For the spinach:

10. In a sauté pan over medium heat, sauté the spinach and garlic in the olive oil. Do not overcook. The heat will continue to wilt the spinach after it is removed from the pan.

TO FINISH THE SALMON:

11. In a large heavy, deep skillet, heat the oil to 375 degrees. It should be hot but not smoking. Fry the fillets until golden on both sides, 4 to 5 minutes. Do not overcook. *Rare is best!* Cut the salmon fillets diagonally in half. If you prefer it cooked all the way through, pop the salmon in the oven (or the microwave works too) and bake it until it is done to your liking.

12. To serve, scoop the potatoes onto the center of each of 4 individual plates. Spoon the spinach around the potatoes. Stand the salmon halves up, back to back, in the mashed potatoes and lay pieces of the fennel over the potatoes and spinach. Sprinkle with toasted sesame seeds.

Note: Substituting a different type of potato for the Idaho is a bad idea because it's more likely to turn gluey when mashed. The exception is the Yukon Gold potato, which actually makes the best mashed potatoes. For this recipe, however, the slightly blander flavor of the Idaho allows the flavor of the salmon and the wasabi to come through with greater force.

SERVES 6

These pots are served at Pongo with a choice of homemade smoked salmon (page 28), grilled shrimp, or scallops. Any meaty white fish, such as halibut or cod, can also be used, and combinations of seafood are good as well. The fresh garnishes add crunch, flavor, and beautiful color.

These are called steam pots because the heat of the broth "steams" the vegetables floating on the top. At Pongo, we make the broth ahead of time and heat it to order in individual pots with wooden handles. (These pots can be purchased inexpensively at most Chinese markets, but a large soup bowl will work just fine, too.) We serve the soup right in the pots.

The amount of seafood you use will depend on whether you're serving this as a first course or an entrée.

BROTH:
- 4 cloves garlic, minced
- 4 shallots, minced
- 2 tablespoons finely grated fresh ginger
- 2 tablespoons olive oil
- Two 13.5-ounce cans coconut milk
- 8 cups fish stock (page 66) or clam juice
- 3 stalks fresh lemongrass, smashed with the flat side of a knife
- 1 teaspoon sugar
- 2 teaspoons Asian fish sauce
- 2 tablespoons minced fresh basil
- 2 tablespoons chopped fresh cilantro
- Dash of red pepper flakes (optional)
- Grated zest of 1 lime (save the lime juice to squeeze over the top just before serving)

SEAFOOD:
- 4 to 8 ounces seafood per person or Pongo's smoked salmon (see Note) (page 28)
- 6 tablespoons oil

NOODLES:
- 1 pound (or more) angel hair pasta, rice noodles, or soba noodles, cooked al dente and cooled to room temperature

GARNISHES
Any combination of the following:
- Sliced scallions
- Julienned carrots
- Julienned red bell pepper
- Bean sprouts
- Radish sprouts
- Lentil sprouts
- Fresh spinach leaves
- Cilantro sprigs
- Basil leaves
- Mint leaves
- Sliced water chestnuts
- Bamboo shoots
- Watercress sprigs
- Arugula leaves
- Shredded Savoy cabbage
- Chopped bok choy
- Toasted sesame seeds (page 130)
- Crushed peanuts
- Fried shallots (page 165)
- Fried sliced garlic
- Juice of 1 lime

For the broth:

1. In a heavy soup pot over medium heat, sauté the garlic, shallots, and ginger in the olive oil until translucent and starting to brown. Add the remaining ingredients. Simmer for 15 minutes.

For the seafood:

2. In individual flameproof pots or in a sauté pan over medium heat brown the seafood of your choice or the Pongo smoked salmon in the olive oil. The seafood does not need to be fully cooked, just browned, as it will simmer in the broth.

To finish the dish:

3. If you are serving in individual pots, ladle the broth into the pots and simmer just until the seafood is cooked all the way through. Make these two at a time; they will hold their heat and more hot broth can be ladled over top. While the pots are piping hot, drop in some noodles. Arrange any combination of the fresh garnishes artfully on top. Squeeze the juice of the lime over the garnishes.

   If you do not have individual pots, scrape the seafood, shallots, and garlic into the broth. Simmer just until the seafood is cooked all the way through. Ladle into bowls. While the soup is still piping hot, drop in the noodles and arrange any combination of the fresh ingredients artfully on top. Finally, add a squeeze of lime. As your guests stir their soup, the fresh garnishes will steam as they are submerged in the hot broth.

Note: The Pongo smoked salmon fillets are outstanding in this dish.

SERVES 4

This may sound simple, but the simplicity of the recipe belies the richness of the finished dish. Its secret is the Worcestershire sauce and balsamic vinegar. Their tart flavors mingle with the sweetness of the tomatoes and red peppers. This sauce and fish are excellent over many types of greens. I recommend collards and mizuna greens with fried garlic. Fresh shelled peas are also a congenial accompaniment.

SAUCE:

2 large onions, minced
6 cloves garlic, sliced
2 tablespoons good-quality olive oil
2 large red bell peppers (overripe is okay)
Two 12-ounce cans Italian plum tomatoes
    with their juice
1 tablespoon Worcestershire sauce
2 tablespoons balsamic vinegar
3 tablespoons minced fresh basil, or
    1 tablespoon dried, plus small sprigs
    for garnish
Cracked black pepper and salt to taste if
    desired

1½ to 2 pounds very fresh halibut, cut
    into 4 to 6 equal pieces, rinsed and
    dried
Grated sharp aged Romano cheese
    (optional)

1. In a large heavy saucepan over medium heat, sauté the onions and garlic in the olive oil until golden. Add the remaining ingredients for the sauce. Cook, stirring occasionally, for about 15 minutes at a steady, bubbling simmer. If you have time, remove the mixture from the heat and let it stand for 1 hour or even overnight. This sauce improves over time.

2. Bring the sauce back to a steady simmer, gently drop in the halibut, and ladle the sauce over the fish. Don't let the fish drift to the bottom but rather let the pieces float in the middle of the sauce. Simmer for about 10 minutes. The cooking time will vary depending on how the thick the fish is cut. The fish is cooked all the way through when it is evenly white and not translucent at the center and flakes apart easily. Divide the fish into individual bowls and garnish with basil sprigs and the Romano.

Salmon Cakes

These cakes can go in many different stylistic directions. The southwestern spin is to serve the salmon cakes with the chipotle rémoulade given here below. The New England direction would be to serve the cakes with an upscale tartar sauce, one that uses capers, instead of pickles, in an aioli (page 119). The Asian variation is to crust the cakes in black and white sesame seeds (or Eden Shake; see page 103) and serve them with pickled ginger slices. Chef's choice.

>1 pound sushi-quality salmon, coarsely
>   chopped
>1 medium onion, chopped
>2 eggs
>1¼ cups Japanese bread crumbs or plain
>   dry bread crumbs
>1 tablespoon rice wine vinegar
>2 tablespoons chopped fresh parsley
>¼ teaspoon salt
>¼ teaspoon cracked pepper
>All-purpose flour for coating
>2 cups vegetable, peanut, or canola oil
>Chipotle Rémoulade (recipe follows)

1. Combine the raw salmon, onion, eggs, bread crumbs, vinegar, parsley, and seasonings. Mix well with your hands.
2. Divide the salmon into 16 equal parts and from these form little cakes shaped like large scallops or hockey pucks. If you prefer the salmon rare in the middle, make the cakes thicker. Refrigerate for 30 minutes.
3. Coat the cakes in flour sprinkled on a plate.
4. In a large, heavy deep skillet over medium heat, heat the oil to 375 degrees. (Test the temperature of the oil by dropping a tiny piece of salmon in the oil. It should brown quickly but not burn.) Fry several of the cakes in the hot oil until golden on both sides, but do not overcook. Rare is best! If you insist that the salmon be cooked all the way through, bake the cakes, after they are fried, in a 300-degree oven for 10 to 15 minutes. Repeat in batches until all the cakes are cooked.
5. Serve hot with the chipotle rémoulade.

Chipotle Rémoulade

     1 cup good-quality mayonnaise or aioli
       (page 119) made without the red
       peppers
     1 teaspoon Dijon mustard
     1 to 2 canned chipotle peppers
     Juice of 1 lime
     1 clove garlic, minced
     1 teaspoon sugar

Put all the ingredients in a food processor or blender and purée until smooth.

SERVES 4 TO 6

"Salpicon" refers to ingredients that are very finely sliced or minced. This dish combines shredded crabmeat with finely minced cilantro and onions. Frozen imitation crabmeat is preferable to cheap crabmeat, which can be dry with the texture and flavor of wood pulp. A blend of lump and imitation can also be used.

For hors d'oeuvres, the blue corn tortillas can be cut into smaller pieces, fried, and served with a spoonful of the salpicon, and minced red onion or sliced avocado on top. Or add some mayonnaise to the chilled salpicon and use it to stuff avocados for a great summer starter.

In the nine years I owned Santa Fe restaurant, reviewers always mentioned these tacos. I recommend serving them with white rice and Santa Fe black beans (page 216)

SALPICON:

1 large Spanish onion, minced
4 cloves garlic, minced
½ fresh jalapeño or serrano pepper (more or less to taste), minced (see page 226)
1½ tablespoons good-quality curry powder
2 tablespoons good-quality olive oil
3 cups fresh lump crabmeat, or frozen imitation crabmeat (see Note)
3 tablespoons minced fresh cilantro, plus small sprigs for garnish

TACOS:

15 to 20 whole blue corn tortillas (not chips)
2 cups or more shredded mild cheese, such as Armenian string cheese, mild Cheddar, or Jack
2 perfectly ripe Hass avocados (see Note)
2 limes
1 head soft leaf lettuce such as red leaf, Bibb, or green leaf, leaves separated, washed, and dried

FOR THE SALPICON:

1. In a large sauté pan over low heat, sauté the onion, garlic, jalapeño, and curry in the oil until the onion is translucent.

2. Add the crabmeat and stir until all is evenly mixed. Lightly brown the mixture over high heat. Stir in the cilantro and remove from the heat.

FOR THE TACOS:

3. Heat a heavy skillet, griddle, or comal over medium to low heat until hot but not smoking. Add as many tortillas as will fit in a single layer.
4. Sprinkle about 2 tablespoons cheese over each tortilla, then layer on about 4 tablespoons of the salpicon.
5. Slowly allow the cheese to melt. Fold the taco over in the pan, allowing the taco to melt closed, and turn it back and forth. When the cheese is completely melted, the tacos are ready.
6. Peel and slice the avocados. Squeeze the juice of 1 of the limes over them so they will hold their color. Plate the tacos, open them, and stuff them with lettuce. Garnish with cilantro series, avocado slices, and the remaining lime cut into thin slices. Serve immediately.

Comal

In Mexico they use a comal, which is simply a cast-iron skillet without sides, to make tacos. If you have one, great! But if like most of the us, you do not, then use any heavy skillet.

Notes: If using frozen imitation crabmeat, allow it to thaw partially. Cut the block into 1-inch strips and grate these using the largest holes of a hand-held grater or the grating disk in a food processor. This process gives the crabmeat a nice texture that allows it to stay in the tacos instead of falling out in big pieces.

Notes: The easiest way to get nice-looking avocado slices is to remove the little stem and cut the avocado in half, starting at the top and going around the pit. Twist open the avocado. While holding the half with the pit in your hand, gently whack the pit with the blade of your knife. When you lift the pit out, it will be stuck to the blade. Whack the blade on the side of the trash can to remove the pit. Cut each avocado half lengthwise in half and peel each quarter with your fingers. Using a sharp knife, cut each quarter into slices.

Prince Edward Island mussels are are grown on ropes in mussel farms. They tend to be medium to small in size, so they are very soft and tender. There are loyal mussel fans who insist that ocean mussels have far better flavor, but they have to be soaked and scrubbed to remove the grit. All the recipes here use the liquid that the mussels are cooked in because they release so much flavor when they are cooking. If you are willing to put in the work, then use any type mussel you prefer; just make sure they are very clean. Beyond the cleaning, have no fear—mussels are very quick and easy to prepare. As Roland says, "Mussels are a party in a bowl." At Pongo, we serve these mussels without pasta as a starter or with pasta as an entrée.

2 cups dry white wine, such as a
    Sauvignon Blanc
6 sprigs parsley
5 sprigs thyme
4 shallots, minced
6 cloves garlic, sliced
Grated zest of 1 lemon
4 cups mussels, cleaned and debearded
2 large ripe tomatoes, chopped
1 pound angel hair pasta, cooked just
    below al dente

1. In a pot large enough to hold all the mussels, add the wine, parsley, thyme, shallots, garlic, and lemon zest and bring to a boil. Drop in the mussels and steam until they open. Quickly pour the liquid into a medium saucepan, add the tomatoes and pasta, and toss over medium heat until the pasta is just warmed through.
2. Have 4 pasta bowls warm and ready. Divide the broth and pasta among the bowls, then add the mussels to each bowl. Serve immediately with crusty bread.

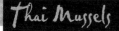
Thai Mussels

This is a perfect appetizer in hot or cold weather.

Two 13.5-ounce cans coconut milk
1 tablespoon green curry paste (available
    at health food stores and Asian
    markets)
1 cup dry white wine, such as a Sauvignon
    Blanc
6 sprigs parsley
4 shallots, minced
6 cloves garlic, sliced
5 sprigs basil
5 sprigs cilantro
Grated zest of 1 lemon
2 large ripe tomatoes, chopped
4 pounds mussels, cleaned and debearded

1. In a pot large enough to hold all the mussels, add all the ingredients except the tomatoes and mussels and bring to a boil. Drop in the mussels and steam until they open. Add the tomatoes and cook no more than a minute longer.
2. Have 4 pasta bowls warm and ready. Divide the broth and the mussels among the bowls. Serve immediately.

Curried Cider Mussels

The flavors of apples and curry combine deliciously with the mussels in this surprising dish.

2 cups good-quality apple cider
1 medium onion, minced
6 cloves garlic, sliced
2 teaspoons good-quality curry powder
Grated zest of 1 lemon
4 pounds mussels, cleaned and debearded

1. In a pot large enough to hold all the mussels, add all the ingredients except the mussels and bring to a boil. Drop in the mussels and steam until they open.
2. Have 4 pasta bowls warm and ready. Divide the broth and then the mussels among the bowls. Serve immediately.

Mussels with White Beans and Spicy Sausage

This variation makes a great supper with crusty bread and beer or a good Chianti.

2 cups dry white wine, such as a
  Sauvignon Blanc
6 sprigs parsley
4 shallots, minced
6 cloves garlic, sliced
5 sprigs thyme
Grated zest of 1 lemon
4 pounds mussels, cleaned and debearded
3 large ripe tomatoes, chopped
2 cups cooked great Northern beans,
  tender but firm to the bite
1 pound spicy Italian sausage, cut into
  1-inch pieces and browned in a skillet
1 pound linguine, cooked just below al
  dente and cooled to room temperature
Grated Parmesan cheese

1. In a pot large enough to hold all the mussels, add the wine, parsley, shallots, garlic, thyme, and lemon zest and bring to a boil. Drop in the mussels and steam until they open. Quickly pour the liquid into a saucepan. Add the tomatoes, beans, sausage, and pasta and toss over medium heat until the pasta is just warmed through.
2. Have 4 pasta bowls warm and ready. Divide the broth and pasta and then the mussels among the bowls. Serve immediately with the Parmesan cheese.

SERVES 4 TO 6

This is a dinner salad. Not that it should be served with dinner, it should be served *for* dinner. The crispy hot calamari slightly wilts the greens and soaks up just the right amount of tangy dressing. It is a perfect summer meal. The salad is best when eaten immediately. If you anticipate guests asking for second helpings, reserve some undressed salad, dressing, and raw calamari and repeat the last two steps of the recipe on demand. Serve green tea ice cream with fortune cookies for dessert.

MISO DRESSING:

¼ cup minced pickled or fresh ginger
¼ cup good-quality white miso paste
7 to 10 scallions, white parts only
2 tablespoons minced garlic
1 cup rice wine vinegar
1 tablespoon good-quality toasted
  sesame oil, preferably Japanese
1 cup peanut, canola, or olive oil

SALAD:

1 head chicory or 2 bunches frisée,
  washed, dried, and torn
1 bunch watercress, large stems trimmed,
  washed, and dried
1 small head radicchio, cored and sliced
1 unpeeled cucumber, julienned
1 carrot, julienned

CALAMARI:

2½ pounds cleaned calamari with tubes
  and tentacles
1 cup milk
2 cups all-purpose flour
½ cup cornstarch
3 cups canola, peanut, or vegetable oil

GARNISH:

1 small red onion
Toasted white or black sesame seeds
  (page 130)
2 limes, halved

For the miso dressing:

1. Combine all the ingredients except the peanut oil in a blender or food processor and blend. Pour into a bowl and slowly whisk in the oil. Set aside.

For the salad:

2. Mix all the ingredients together. The salad can be kept in a plastic bag in the refrigerator until ready to serve. When about ready to serve, put the salad in a very large bowl.

For the calamari:

3. Cut the calamari tubes into ¼-inch rings. Cut any large tentacle clusters in half. Cover the calamari with the milk until ready to fry.

4. Heat the oil to 375 degrees in a wok or the largest cast-iron skillet or heavy pot you have. Mix the flour and cornstarch on a *platter*. When everything else is completely ready and your guests are sitting at the table, begin to fry. Have the salad bowl, dressing, large dinner plates, garnish, and salad tongs near you. Dust about 1 cup of the calamari with the flour mixture and shake off any excess. This is done easily by standing over a trash can with a wire basket or colander and tapping the excess flour into the garbage. Fry the calamari until it is light golden brown. Do not overcook or it will become rubbery.

5. With a slotted spoon, scoop the hot calamari right into the salad. Working quickly, fry the next batch. Immediately toss the salad with enough of the dressing to just coat the leaves lightly.

6. Quickly plate the salads, dividing the calamari evenly. Garnish each plate with onion slices, sesame seeds, and a big squeeze of fresh lime juice.

SERVES 4 TO 6

This is a very simple recipe to make. The chicken roasts at 200 degrees for four hours. The slow cooking makes for the moistest bird you'll ever taste. Total *preparation* time is about ten minutes. The long cooking time is perfect if there are errands to run or gardening to do. I prepare, cook, and serve this chicken in the same cast-iron skillet. When the chicken is done, set the table, make a salad (perhaps chicory and red leaf lettuce with pecans and an apple cider vinaigrette), and you're finished.

1 garlic bulb
4 tablespoons butter
4 tablespoons olive oil
3 rosemary sprigs, leaves removed from
    stems
1 large Spanish or Vidalia onion, cut into
    ¼-inch half-moon slices
2 apples, such as Gala, Jonagold, or
    Golden Delicious, cored and cut into
    quarters
2 unpeeled oranges, cut into quarters
2 small sweet potatoes or 1 large, washed
    and cut into 1½-inch circles
1 whole 4- to 6-pound chicken, giblets
    are welcome
Salt and cracked pepper to taste

1. Preheat the oven to 200 degrees.
2. Cut the bulb of garlic in half. Peel half the cloves and mash them into a paste. Leave the other half in whole cloves with their skins.
3. In a small bowl, mash the butter with a fork into 2 tablespoons of the olive oil and the garlic paste. Add the rosemary, salt, and pepper. Rub this mixture all over the inside and outside of the chicken. Rub the remainder in a large cast-iron skillet.
4. Place the onion, apples, oranges, sweet potatoes, and the whole garlic cloves in the pan and drizzle them with the remaining 2 tablespoons olive oil. Place the chicken on top. Salt and pepper the whole pot.

5. Roast for 4 hours. Increase the oven temperature to 500 degrees and cook until the chicken is golden brown, about 15 to 20 minutes. Stir the fruit up from the bottom at least once or twice so it can evenly brown. The chicken is done when the legs move freely and the meat is not translucent pink near the bone. A meat thermometer inserted into the chicken should read no more than 165 degrees.

6. Serve the chicken in the skillet. Carve at the table.

SERVES 4

This dish has wonderful sweet and tangy flavors. The chicken with the figs must marinate overnight. I make this chicken a lot for dinner parties in the fall and winter. Oven-roasted Brussels sprouts or roasted winter vegetables (page 212 or 211) are a great complement.

1/2 cup (packed) brown sugar
1/4 cup olive oil
1 cup Spanish olives with their juice
1 cup figs soaked in sweet vermouth
  (page 223)
1/2 cup of the vermouth
6 cloves garlic, minced
1 teaspoon cracked black pepper
1 teaspoon sea salt
1 teaspoon red pepper flakes
2 tablespoons distilled white vinegar
1 tablespoon Dijon mustard
1 tablespoon minced fresh oregano
1 tablespoon fresh thyme leaves
2 bay leaves
1 whole 4- to 6-pound chicken, cut into
  quarters

1. Combine all the ingredients and let sit in a covered bowl in the refrigerator overnight.
2. Preheat the oven to 250 degrees.
3. Bake the chicken with the marinade in a shallow baking dish for about 2 hours. Baste the chicken a few times as it bakes. When the thigh releases clear juices, the chicken is done. A meat thermometer inserted into the chicken should read 175 degrees. Be careful. Overcooking will result in dry chicken. Serve on an attractive platter.

Barbecued Lemon Chicken with Crushed Cumin and Coriander Seeds

This is an easy recipe for melt-in-your-mouth barbecued chicken. I've found that the easiest way to crush dry seeds is in a coffee grinder; buy a second one so that you don't unintentionally flavor your coffee beans! Despite what you may think, unseasoned meat tenderizer is pure, natural, and devoid of such horrors as MSG. It is, essentially, dried papain, which is an enzyme that occurs naturally in the papaya and has the wondrous quality of tenderizing meat. While it's a bit messier and requires more preparation, sliced papaya will work just as well in this marinade.

Serve this with Toasted Mustard Seed Slaw (page 215).

1 whole 4- to 6-pound chicken, quartered
3 tablespoons freshly crushed or ground
    cumin seeds
3 tablespoons freshly crushed or ground
    coriander seeds
6 cloves garlic, minced
2 tablespoons unseasoned meat
    tenderizer, or 1 papaya, peeled
    and sliced
Salt and cracked pepper to taste
1/2 cup olive oil
2 lemons, cut into wedges
Coarsely chopped fresh cilantro for
    garnish

1. With a sharp knife, make diagonal slashes 1 inch apart in the chicken pieces.
2. Rub the chicken pieces all over with the cumin, coriander, half the garlic, the meat tenderizer (or some of the papaya—here's where it can get messy), salt, and pepper, making sure that the ingredients get rubbed into the slashes in the chicken. In a large bowl, toss the chicken pieces with the olive oil, remaining garlic, and remaining papaya if you've chosen that over the meat tenderizer. Squeeze the lemon wedges over the chicken, then throw them in the bowl and toss the mixture once again.
3. Let the chicken marinate for at least 1 hour in the refrigerator (a few hours is better for really melding the flavors), turning the pieces periodically in the marinade.
4. Grill the chicken slowly over low heat, keeping the barbecue covered except to turn the chicken pieces (which you should do frequently for even cooking). Garnish with fresh cilantro.

SERVES 4 TO 7

This recipe comes from the other side of the river. Although the river crossing is about thirty minutes from town to town, there are two separate worlds. The Rosendale people have heard about the Tivoli people and vice versa, but rarely do the two worlds collide—like the Montagues and the Capulets. Rosendale exists as Tivoli's parallel universe. Jack and I met at a party on neutral turf. He had brought some food from his café, including this amazing chicken in a very dark and incredibly yummy sauce. My interest was piqued. We spent the remainder of the party talking about food and life in a small-town café. We now collaborate on catered events. In a gesture of extreme kindness and generosity, Jack gave me this recipe. It was among his most cherished cooking secrets; when you try it you'll see why. This recipe makes a bit more sauce than you'll need, but it is a great thing to have around for veggies or as a dipping sauce. Jack also recommends trying it on chicken wings. Overnight marinating of the chicken is recommended.

SAUCE:
- 1/4 cup Chinese fermented black beans
- 1/2 cup soy sauce
- 1/4 cup toasted sesame oil
- 1/4 cup rice wine vinegar
- 1/2 cup packed brown sugar
- 1/4 cup molasses
- 2/3 cup hoisin sauce
- 1/4 cup horseradish
- 1/4 cup Dijon mustard
- 2 tablespoons sambal oelek or red pepper flakes, or more to taste
- 2 tablespoons minced garlic
- 1/2 cup ketchup

CHICKEN:
- One 4- to 7-pound chicken, cut into quarters, or 4 pounds chicken wings

1. Combine all the ingredients for the sauce in a mixing bowl
2. Toss the raw chicken parts with about half the sauce, enough so that it is well coated. Marinate in the refrigerator at least 6 hours, but preferably overnight.
3. Preheat the oven to 400 degrees.
4. Roast the chicken on a baking sheet for about 25 minutes per pound. Turn and baste the chicken with the remaining sauce about every 15 minutes. You may not use all the sauce, so be careful not to contaminate it with the basting brush that has touched the uncooked chicken. Pour a little at a time into a separate bowl as you baste.

Red Curried Chicken with Ginger-Infused Basmati Rice

SERVES 4

This recipe tastes best when the chicken is marinated overnight. If you can plan ahead for that, the rest is smooth sailing. Steamed spinach would be a good complement to this dish.

> ½ cup coarsely chopped fresh basil, plus
>   small sprigs for garnish
> 6 cloves garlic, minced
> 1 tablespoon red curry paste (available at
>   health food stores and Asian markets)
> ½ cup olive oil
> ¼ cup red wine vinegar
> 4 medium-size whole skinless, boneless
>   chicken breasts
> Ginger-Infused Basmati Rice (page 160)

1. Mix the basil, garlic, red curry paste, olive oil, and vinegar together. Pour over the chicken and marinate in a covered container at least 6 hours, but preferably overnight, in the refrigerator.
2. Preheat the oven to 375 degrees. Place the chicken with all the marinade in a cast-iron skillet or shallow baking dish. Bake the chicken breasts for 20 to 30 minutes until the breasts are firm. When you cut into the breast, there should be no pink. Do not overcook.
3. Start the rice immediately after the chicken goes in the oven; they will be ready at about the same time.
4. Scoop the rice into the center of an attractive platter. Move the rice toward the edges, creating space in the center. Scoop the chicken into the center of the rice. Garnish with small basil sprigs. Serve immediately.

SERVES 4

The mushroom-cheese mixture I call Mushroom "Boursin" is used quite a bit at the Café Pongo. I like having it around. If you have the mixture made ahead of time, this recipe is very quick and simple to make.

Serve with a mixed green salad and a freshly baked baguette.

> 4 large skinless, boneless chicken breast
>   halves
> 1/2 cup mushroom boursin (page 136)
> 8 thin slices prosciutto
> 2 tablespoons olive oil
> 1/2 cup all-purpose flour
> Salt and cracked pepper to taste
> 1 cup chicken stock, homemade (page 67)
>   or canned
> 1/2 cup balsamic vinegar
> 4 cloves garlic, sliced
> 1 bay leaf
> 1 tablespoon fresh thyme leaves, plus
>   sprigs for garnish
> 2 tablespoons butter

1. Butterfly the chicken breasts: Slice them horizontally almost all the way through so that they open like a book. Lay 2 slices of prosciutto inside each breast and cover with the "Boursin." Pinch the breasts shut to make sure that none of the filling leaks out.

2. Heat the olive oil in a heavy skillet over medium heat. Season the flour on a plate with salt and pepper. Coat the stuffed chicken breasts with the seasoned flour. Brown the chicken breasts in the olive oil on both sides. Add the chicken broth, vinegar, garlic, bay leaf, and fresh thyme. Simmer for 10 minutes, turning the chicken breasts for even cooking.

3. Remove the chicken from the pan and simmer the sauce over low heat, stirring regularly to prevent sticking, until it is reduced and thickened (5 to 10 minutes). Whisk in the butter until it melts.

4. Arrange the chicken breasts on a platter and pour the sauce over them. Garnish with fresh thyme sprigs.

Stewed Chicken with Kalamata Olives, Sun-Dried Tomatoes, and Pan-Seared Penne

I highly recommend serving this chicken with a chicory salad. The slightly bitter crunch of the greens perfectly complements the pan-seared pasta and sweet tang of the chicken. Toss the chicory with olive oil and balsamic vinegar and serve the salad on the same plate as the chicken.

PASTA:

1 pound penne pasta
1 tablespoon olive oil
2 tablespoons butter
2 shallots, minced

CHICKEN:

5 tablespoons olive oil
12 chicken thighs
1½ cups all-purpose flour
5 cloves garlic, minced
2 shallots, minced
2 cups dry red wine
¾ cup pitted Kalamata olives, with
   2 tablespoons of their brine
1½ cups sliced sun-dried tomatoes
1 tablespoon fresh thyme leaves
2 tablespoons chopped fresh basil
2 tablespoons balsamic vinegar
Salt and cracked pepper to taste

Shaved romano cheese for serving
Small thyme or basil sprigs for garnish

FOR THE PASTA:

1. Cook the penne in a large pot of boiling water until al dente. Pour it into a colander and cool it completely under cold running water. Toss the penne with the olive oil to keep it from sticking.

FOR THE CHICKEN:

2. In a large sauté pan, heat 4 tablespoons of the olive oil over high heat. Roll the chicken thighs in the flour, add to the pan, and brown on both sides. If there is not room in the skillet for all the chicken pieces at once, brown the pieces in batches. The chicken will be fully cooked when it simmers in the

red wine. When all the chicken is browned on both sides, return it to the skillet.

3. Add the garlic and shallots to the chicken and stir until the shallots start to become translucent. Add the remaining ingredients and simmer over low heat for at least 20 minutes. Cut into a piece to make sure it is cooked all the way through.

4. To pan-sear the pasta, heat 1 tablespoon of the butter in a large nonstick skillet over medium heat. Add a single layer of penne and let the pasta turn golden brown on the bottom. Drop in some of the shallots. Continue to cook until the pasta is crisp on at least one side and the shallots are translucent. Remove the pasta and shallots from the pan and repeat with the remaining butter, penne, and shallots.

5. To serve, divide the pasta among 6 plates and top with a ladle of stewed chicken. Garnish with shaved Romano, cracked pepper, and thyme sprigs.

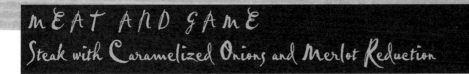
SERVES 4

This is a very simple and fairly quick way to dress up a steak. We serve it on a bed of sautéed kale with either mashed potatoes with broiled Gruyère on top, or with Swiss potatoes (page 218). The method for cooking steak was taught to me by my first love. (He also introduced me to balsamic vinegar.) This method is the key to making very rare (black and blue) steak. It has that thick dark crust that sets a good steak apart. If you stubbornly prefer your meat well done, then the method and the cut are less important. Boiling will work fine.

MERLOT REDUCTION:

> 8 onions, sliced ¼ inch thick
> 2 tablespoons olive oil
> 4 cups Merlot
> 6 sprigs thyme, stems removed
> 1 teaspoon sugar
> 2 tablespoons butter

STEAK:

> 1 tablespoon kosher salt
> Four 8- to 16-ounce steaks, cut 1½ to
>   2½ inches thick (anything from New
>   York strip to filet mignon will do)

FOR THE MERLOT REDUCTION:

1. In a heavy cast-iron skillet over low heat, cook the sliced onions in the oil until they are completely soft, sweet, and caramelized, 30 to 40 minutes. Stir them occasionally. If the onions stick or burn at all, the flame is too high (see page 137).

2. Add the wine, thyme, and sugar to the onions. Simmer over low heat until the wine is reduced in volume by about a quarter.

FOR THE STEAK

3. Scatter the kosher salt over the bottom of a cast-iron skillet and heat over high heat. (Either use 2 skillets or wash the one you have after you've cooked the first 2 steaks.) Let the pan get so hot that it is smoking. Press 2 steaks into the pan. Do not move the steak until a dark (not quite black) crust has formed on the bottom. The amount of time you cook the second side will determine the doneness of the meat. For rare, the second side hardly cooks at all.

4. When the steaks are done, bring the sauce to a simmer and whisk in the butter. Serve the steaks dark side up with the sauce both on top and pooled around the meat.

Note: Cooking steak this way makes a lot of smoke. If you do not have a good exhaust fan, open some windows.

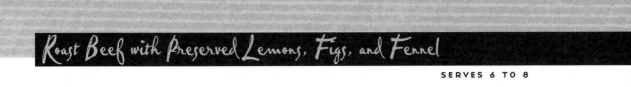
Preserved lemons need to sit for about one week. The figs need to sit at least overnight. Both of these items have many uses and are well worth having around. This roast can be served hot, right out of the oven, or sliced and served cold for lunch. The onions and the fennel absorb the intricate flavors of the soaked figs and the salty lemons. This seems like the sort of dish that Leonardo da Vinci might have brought to a potluck.

> One 4- to 5-pound beef of round eye roast
> Kosher salt and cracked pepper
> 1 tablespoon olive oil
> 1 garlic bulb, cloves smashed and peeled
> 3 cups figs in sweet vermouth with all their juice (page 223)
> 2 cups Preserved Lemons (recipe follows), rinsed
> 1 large Spanish onion, or 2 medium onions, unpeeled, cut into 1/4-inch-thick half-moon slices
> 6 rosemary sprigs, plus a few sprigs for garnish
> 8 thyme sprigs
> 2 tablespoons minced fresh oregano
> 2 fennel bulbs, cut into 1/2-inch wedges

1. Preheat the oven to 250 degrees.
2. Rub the roast with salt and pepper. In a cast-iron skillet over high heat brown the roast in the oil on all sides. It should take about 20 minutes. Remove the pan from the heat and the roast from the pan. Combine all the remaining ingredients in the pan and stir until they are evenly coated with the liquids. Nestle the roast back in the pan and roast covered for about 2 hours. Uncover and raise the heat to 450 degrees for the last 10 to 15 minutes. Turn the roast and stir the vegetables about every 30 minutes. Cooking time is not exact. The most accurate way to determine doneness is with an instant-read thermometer. Rare is around 135 degrees. (For an outstanding cut of beef, the temperature can be as low as 120 degrees, but most of us do not like our round roast black and blue.) If you insist on completely killing it, 185 degrees is well done. If a meat thermometer is not available, use the trim and nibble technique: Cut the edges of the roast. If the edges are rare, the center

is raw. When the edges are a pink medium, the center is usually perfect. (If it is too rare, you can always throw it back in the oven.) Once the meat is out of the oven, let it stand for 5 minutes covered with foil before slicing. Serve on a platter with the figs, lemons, and garlic. Garnish with rosemary sprigs.

Preserved Lemons

YIELDS ABOUT 1 QUART

6 scrubbed lemons, cut into quarters
2 cups kosher salt
1 cup sugar
3 tablespoons whole cloves

1. Combine all the ingredients in a clean dry jar or Tupperware container. The container must have a tight-fitting lid and be roomy enough to shake up the ingredients; otherwise all the salt and sugar will settle to the bottom.
2. For the first week, shake the contents of your lemon container every day. After the first week or so, the lemons will release their juice and the container will be filled with clear liquid. This indicates the lemons are ready to be used for cooking. The lemons will keep for an indefinite amount of time if they are not contaminated by dirty utensils. Rinse the lemons before cooking with them.

SERVES 4

Pork tenderloin is the same cut as beef filet mignon. This is a tender and lean cut of meat that is also simple to prepare. Despite age-old fears, pork tenderloin *can* be eaten medium rare to medium. Some pink *is* fine. There is no need to cook it until it is dried out.

The tenderloin can be served hot or cold. The pesto has a toasted nutty flavor that is well matched with the tang of the tomatillos. Cilantro haters need not apply. The tenderloins are better if they can marinate overnight, but you can get away with 4 hours.

PORK:

> 2 pork tenderloins, 8 to 12 ounces each
> 1 bottle golden beer
> 1 garlic bulb, minced
> 2 tablespoons olive oil
> Cracked pepper

PESTO:

> 1/2 cup hulled green pumpkin seeds
> 3/4 cup good-quality olive oil
> 12 tomatillos, husked and rinsed
> 1 cup (packed) fresh cilantro leaves
> 1 tablespoon sugar
> Juice of 1 lime
> 3 cloves garlic, peeled
> Avocado slices, lime slices, and cilantro
>   sprigs for garnish

TO FINISH THE DISH:

> 1 tablespoon kosher salt

FOR THE PORK:

1. In the refrigerator, marinate the tenderloins in the beer with the minced garlic, olive oil, and pepper for 4 to 24 hours. Use a small enough container so that the beer covers the pork.

FOR THE PESTO:

2. In a cast-iron skillet over medium heat, toast the pumpkin seeds in the olive oil until they are golden brown.
3. Scrape the seeds with the oil into a food processor. Return the skillet to the stove and sear the tomatillos over high heat. Do not cook them until they soften; simply move them around the pan until they darken on two sides.

4. While the tomatillos are in the pan, purée the cilantro with the pumpkin seeds. Add the sugar, lime juice, and garlic and purée again. Add the tomatillos and purée until smooth.

TO FINISH THE DISH:

5. Sprinkle a cast-iron skillet with the kosher salt and heat over high heat. Add the tenderloins and brown on all sides until they are dark and crusty. Reduce the heat to medium and cook to desired doneness. The meat will be served sliced, so do not be afraid to cut into the fattest part and have a peek. A meat thermometer should read 150 to 155 degrees. Let the meat sit covered with foil for about 5 minutes before slicing. The temperature will then increase a little. Slice the tenderloins on a diagonal.

6. To serve, spoon the pesto onto 4 individual plates. Arrange the pork slices on top. Garnish with avocado slices (see page 177 for advice on making perfect slices), lime slices, and cilantro sprigs.

SERVES 4

This is a cozy winter dish that can be prepared and served in the same cast-iron skillet. It is very simple to prepare but elegant enough for company. I recommend serving it with blanched green beans and a chicory salad with an apple-cider vinegar dressing. Oven-roasted cabbage with caraway seeds or sweet potatoes baked with maple butter and fresh rosemary would also be good.

> 4 center-cut ³/₄-inch-thick pork chops,
>   bone in or boneless
> Cracked pepper
> Kosher salt
> 4 thyme sprigs, plus some sprigs for
>   garnish
> 1 Spanish onion, diced
> 2 Granny Smith apples, cored and cut into
>   thick slices
> 2 cups chicken stock (page 67)
> ¹/₂ cup dry white wine
> 5 cloves garlic, smashed and peeled
> 2 tablespoons Dijon mustard
> 2 tablespoons whole-grain mustard
> 1 cup heavy cream

1. Preheat the oven to 350 degrees.
2. Season the chops with cracked pepper. Using a cast-iron skillet that is large enough to brown all 4 chops, sprinkle the bottom of the pan with kosher salt. Heat the skillet over medium-high heat until it is starting to smoke. Add the chops and brown on both sides. Remove from the heat. Slide the thyme sprigs under the chops and cover the chops with the onion and apples. Add the chicken stock, wine, and garlic to the pan. Cover with aluminum foil and bake for 30 minutes.
3. Remove the foil. In a small bowl, whisk the mustards into the cream and pour over the chops. Bake uncovered for another 20 minutes. Garnish with fresh thyme sprigs.

Saddle of Venison with Sun-Dried Cherry Merlot Reduction

I served this venison at a recent fall wedding, which took place in a corn field. Beautiful paper lanterns hung at different heights all around the tent. Ballroom chairs, rich chocolate linens, tapestries, and beautiful fall foliage completed the setting. The menu equally matched the season: Rosemary garlic chicken roasted with local apples, onions, and clementines; roasted root vegetables and pan-seared Belgian endive and fennel. Pomegranate, pear, and Stilton were tossed into the salad. But the dish that received the most praise was the venison.

After the cherries simmer in the reduced wine and stock, they develop a sweet earthy taste that matches the musky flavor of the venison. Try to convince your meat purveyor to trim the silver skin from the venison saddle; this is a tedious job. If the meat is trimmed and you leave an extra day for marinating, this dish is *fairly* simple.

VENISON:

8 ounces sliced bacon
1 trimmed venison saddle, 2 to 4 pounds,
    preferably farm-raised (see Note)
1 tablespoon kosher salt

MARINADE:

1 cup olive oil
6 cloves garlic, smashed and peeled
1 cup Merlot
Cracked pepper to taste

SAUCE:

6 cups pork or beef stock (page 67)
4 cups Merlot
4 thyme sprigs, plus sprigs for garnish
1 rosemary sprig, plus sprigs for garnish
1 cup sun-dried cherries
1/2 cup maple syrup
2 tablespoons Worcestershire sauce
1/2 cup (1 stick) butter
Salt and cracked pepper to taste

FOR THE VENISON:

1. Wrap the raw bacon around the venison saddle. Sprinkle the kosher salt on a flat griddle or over the bottom of a cast-iron skillet and heat over medium to high heat until the griddle begins to smoke. Place the bacon-wrapped saddle on the griddle and brown on all sides. Remember the meat is not being cooked, just browned. Discard the bacon or make BLTs (page 107) with it.

FOR THE MARINADE:

2. Rub the browned meat first with the olive oil and then the garlic in a deep pan or bowl. Add the red wine and cracked pepper. Let marinate overnight in the refrigerator.
3. When ready to cook the venison, preheat the oven to 400 degrees.
4. Remove the venison from the marinade. Roast the venison in a roasting pan until a meat thermometer inserted in the thickest part reads between 130 and 140 degrees, about 40 minutes. The meat should have some color. Once it turns gray, it's overcooked. Let stand, covered with foil, for 15 minutes before slicing.

FOR THE SAUCE:

5. While the venison is roasting, simmer the stock and wine with the thyme and rosemary in a heavy saucepan until the liquid is reduced to less than one-third its original volume.
6. Strain the reduction and add the cherries, maple syrup, and Worcestershire. Simmer until the cherries are plump and the sauce has thickened. Drop in the butter and season with salt and pepper to taste. Stir occasionally until the butter is melted.
7. Slice the venison and serve with the sauce poured over the top and garnished with herb sprigs.

Note: The venison can be ordered from Highland Farm, 283 County Rte. 6, Germantown, NY 12526. Phone: 518-537-6397.

6

SIDES AND CONDIMENTS

*E*very great entrée deserves a great side dish, which should be chosen that day from what looks beautiful at the market. Toss butter and honey with young spring carrots; cool a grilled summer chicken with a cold radish salad, when you find them fresh and bright red with the greens still attached. In winter discover turnips, parsnips, and squash. I often decide what to make for dinner by first picking my sides.

SERVES 4

This crisp summer salad is unusual and refreshing. It complements grilled fish and chicken. If you can't find Eden Shake, substitute equal parts toasted sesame seeds and nori flakes and dulce flakes. If you don't have daikon radish, the salad is just as good with three bunches of summer's best beautiful red radishes.

2 bunches red radishes
8 ounces daikon radish (half a medium
   daikon)

DRESSING:

¼ cup rice wine vinegar
½ cup olive oil
1 tablespoon thinly slivered fresh mint
1 tablespoon chopped fresh cilantro
1 tablespoon chopped fresh flat-leaf
   parsley
1 tablespoon Eden Shake
Radish sprouts and mint sprigs for garnish

1. Slice the radishes, then quarter the slices to make little triangular pieces. As the radishes are being cut and as the dressing is made, keep the sliced radishes in an ice bath to prevent them from getting limp and turning brown.

2. In a separate bowl, whisk all the ingredients for the dressing together. Drain the radishes and toss them with the dressing. Keep chilled until ready to serve. Garnish with a tuft of radish sprouts and mint sprigs. Do not sprinkle with the sprouts until the very end; otherwise they will get mushy.

Lady Jane's Carrot Salad

My close friend Jane showed me this recipe in college. Jane is from London, a city with a large Indian population, so she was familiar with many ingredients which at that time (1986) were hard to find in the United States. I had never heard of more than one mustard seed, but once I tasted this salad I was hooked. Now these little seeds are an essential element in my spice rack. I used to have to hunt for them, but today they're much more readily available.

> ¹/₄ cup olive oil
> 2 tablespoons black mustard seeds
> 6 large carrots, peeled and grated
> Juice of 1 lemon

In a small covered skillet over medium heat, heat the oil and the mustard seeds. Allow the mustard seeds to "pop" like popcorn as they heat in the oil. When the popping subsides (about 2 minutes), pour the hot oil and seeds over the carrots. Toss the carrots, oil, and mustard seeds together with the lemon juice.

Sicilian Cauliflower with Anchovies

This fresh approach to cauliflower always receives a lot of compliments at catered events. It can be served hot or at room temperature and tastes great the next day.

> 1 medium head cauliflower, broken into
> whole florets about 2 inches long
> 3 tablespoons good-quality olive oil
> 4 cloves garlic, minced
> 1 teaspoon red pepper flakes
> 1 to 3 anchovey fillets, depending on
> size of the fillets and your taste for
> anchovies
> Salt to taste
> 1/4 cup coarsely chopped fresh flat-leaf
> parsley

1. Steam the cauliflower pieces until they are al dente—firm but not crunchy.
2. Put the olive oil, garlic, pepper flakes, and anchovies in a large pan, skillet, or wok. Mashing the anchovies with the back of a fork, sauté until the garlic is translucent.
3. Add the steamed cauliflower and stir to coat it fully with the oil mixture. Add salt but taste carefully as the anchovies themselves add saltiness to the dish. Cook long enough to brown a few of the edges of the florets. Be careful not to overcook the cauliflower and burn the garlic.
4. Place the cauliflower in a warmed serving dish and toss with the parsley.

Butter-Roasted Beets

Beets are a love-hate kind of vegetable. I love them any style: boiled, roasted, raw. Therefore, they are regularly served at Pongo. Customers often comment that they have always hated beets but really like ours. This is because we roast them. This changes the texture and flavor just enough to gain a few converts to the beet team.

> 3 tablespoons butter
> 6 medium beets, peeled and cut into
>   1-inch pieces
> Salt to taste

1. Preheat the oven to 350 degrees.
2. Cut the butter into small pieces and mix with the cut-up beets and salt in a bowl. Pour this mixture onto a baking sheet or in a roasting pan. Roast until soft and a bit browned but not mushy, about 20 minutes, stirring occasionally. Serve hot.

Pan-Seared Belgian Endive

SERVES 4

When most people think of Belgian endive, they imagine eating it raw. At Pongo, we serve it this way too. However, my favorite Belgian endive is slowly cooked and served hot. It tastes sweeter and delivers more of its subtle flavors when the bitter edge is removed. Endive also has a really beautiful shape when sliced in half. I often lay it around a roast on a serving tray.

> 8 Belgian endives (choose the smaller ones)
> 2 to 3 tablespoons good-quality extra-virgin olive oil

1. Remove just the very end of each endive stump and remove any loose outer leaves. Carefully cut the endives lengthwise in half.
2. In a cast-iron skillet or heavy sauté pan, heat the olive oil over medium to low heat. Lay the endives flat side down in the olive oil and cook until deep golden brown on the underside. Carefully roll the endives over and cook the other side, about 7 minutes on each side.

Braised Butter Honey Carrots

SERVES 4

I recommend using thin small carrots, peeled and cut on a diagonal, or those carrots that come already peeled and bagged cut lengthwise in half. Browning the butter gives it a deep smoky flavor that complements the sweetness of the carrots and honey.

> 4 cups sliced ($1/4$ to $1/2$ inch) carrots
> 2 tablespoons butter
> 1 tablespoon honey

1. In a medium pan, drop the carrots into 5 to 6 cups boiling water and boil for 2 to 3 minutes. Drain well.
2. Heat the butter in a heavy sauté pan large enough to hold the carrots in a single layer over low heat until the butter turns deep golden brown. Immediately drop in the carrots, add the honey, and stir until all of the carrots are evenly coated.

Spaghetti Squash with Plum Tomatoes and Garlic

This dish is very quick and simple, qualities not suggested by how delicious it is.

> 1 medium spaghetti squash
> One 28-ounce can fancy plum tomatoes
>   with their juice
> 4 cloves garlic, minced
> Salt and cracked pepper to taste
> 2 tablespoons good-quality extra-virgin
>   olive oil
> Grated Parmesan cheese (optional)

1. Preheat the oven to 350 degrees.
2. Cut the squash lengthwise in half. Seed it and lay it cut side up in a baking pan. If you cut a small slice from the bottom side, it will prevent the squash from rolling, but do not cut so deep that the center cavity will leak.
3. Mix the tomatoes, garlic, salt, and pepper, crushing the tomatoes with your hands (or chop them). Divide the mixture equally between the squash halves. Pour 1 tablespoon olive oil into each half.
4. Bake until the squash can be gently pulled away from the sides, about 35 minutes. Serve the squash family-style in its shell, scooping the spaghetti-like strands onto each plate. (It may be helpful to loosen the inside of the squash with a fork before serving.) Sprinkle Parmesan cheese on top before serving.

Shoestring Parsnips

This side dish is quick and very simple to prepare. Crispy and utterly delicious, it is the perfect complement to the butternut squash risotto (page 165). At Pongo we serve these parsnips with many dishes, including salads and pasta. If decadence is your game, use rendered duck fat for this dish. The parsnips would be perfect served with duck.

8 to 12 parsnips, peeled
2 tablespoons olive oil or rendered
    duck fat

1. Preheat the oven to 400 degrees.
2. Cut the parsnips lengthwise in half. Lay them down on their flat sides and cut lengthwise into slices about as thick as a fast-food French fry.
3. Spread the parsnips on a baking sheet, drizzle them with the oil, and toss them a couple of times. Roast the parsnips until tender, 30 to 35 minutes. Every 10 to 15 minutes, give the pan a shake, gently loosening any stuck pieces. The parts that get brown and crispy are the best.
4. Serve hot.

Roasted Winter Vegetables with Fresh Thyme

This dish always reminds me just how many wonderful vegetables there are available in the winter. We always have a seasonal vegetable on the menu at Pongo. When Roland started making this, I anticipated the coming of spring just a little less intensely.

All the vegetables should be cut into fairly uniform pieces so they cook evenly and look good together.

1 cup chopped celery
1 cup chopped turnips
1 cup chopped fennel
1 cup peeled and chopped carrots
1 cup peeled and chopped parsnips
2 cups peeled and chopped Hubbard or
    other winter squash
1/4 cup olive oil
2 tablespoons fresh thyme leaves, plus
    small sprigs for garnish
Salt and cracked pepper to taste
2 tablespoons butter
2 cups peeled and chopped beets

1. Preheat the oven to 375 degrees.
2. Toss all the vegetables except the beets with the olive oil and thyme. Spread the vegetables in a single layer in a roasting pan and season with salt and pepper. Roast until soft but not mushy (20 minutes). Stir only when you see the vegetables starting to overbrown. The parts that get brown and crispy are the best.
3. In a separate pan, melt the butter. Add the beets, toss to coat, and roast until soft but not mushy, 20 to 25 minutes.
4. In a serving dish, put the roasted mixed vegetables in the center, piling them high, and arrange the beets in a ring around them. Garnish with the thyme sprigs.

The pungent flavors of the citrus and sage lend themselves well to the wonderful, almost musty, flavor of Brussels sprouts. The toasted chestnuts add a textural complexity that complements the other ingredients.

1 pint Brussels sprouts
1 tablespoon olive oil
1 tablespoon butter
6 chestnuts, boiled, peeled, and coarsely
   chopped (see Note)
1 tablespoon finely slivered sage leaves
1 teaspoon grated lemon zest
Salt and cracked pepper to taste

1. Preheat the oven to 350 degrees.
2. Remove the loose outer leaves of the Brussels sprouts. Trim the stems and score each one with an X on the bottom.
3. Add the oil to the Brussels sprouts in a cast-iron skillet and toss to coat. Roast until tender, 15 to 20 minutes. Transfer the Brussels sprouts to a serving dish.
4. Place the skillet over low heat. Put the butter and chestnuts in the skillet (no need to change pans or wash the one you're using). Sauté until the chestnuts are golden brown.
5. Return the Brussels sprouts to the pan with the sage, lemon zest, salt, and pepper and sauté briefly until everything is mixed and the flavors are blended, 1 to 2 minutes. Serve hot.

Note: To prepare the chestnuts, score an X in the flat side of each nut with a sharp knife. Drop into a pot of boiling water and boil for 5 minutes. Drain, and peel the outer shell and inner papery covering while the nuts are still warm.

Sesame Green Beans with Crispy Onions

This salad is best eaten while the onions are still hot. As soon as it is tossed, the tangy dressing soaks into the crispy onions for really satisfying texture as well as flavor. The red pepper adds color.

GREEN BEANS:

> 8 cups fresh green beans, stems removed
> 1/2 red bell pepper, cut into strips
> 1 tablespoon olive oil
> 1 tablespoon toasted sesame oil
> 1/2 teaspoon red pepper flakes, or more
>   to taste

ONIONS:

> 2 cups vegetable, peanut, or canola oil
> 1 cup all-purpose flour
> Salt and cracked pepper
> 1 medium onion, sliced thin
> 2 tablespoons sesame seeds, toasted
>   (page 130)
> 2 tablespoons rice wine vinegar
> Juice of 1 lemon

1. Preheat the oven to 400 degrees.

FOR THE GREEN BEANS:

2. Toss the green beans and red pepper strips with the olive oil, sesame oil, and red pepper flakes. Roast these in a single layer in a shallow baking pan for 8 to 10 minutes. Taste a bean or two for desired crispness.

FOR THE ONIONS:

3. Heat the oil in a large, deep, heavy skillet over medium heat (375 degrees). Season the flour with salt and pepper. Coat the onion slices evenly with the flour and fry in the oil until golden brown. Drain on a paper towel.

4. While the onions are still hot, toss them with the green beans, sesame seeds, rice wine vinegar, and lemon juice. Serve at once.

I come from a long line of slaw lovers. We are so dedicated to this cabbage delicacy that my brother and I even enjoy the overly sweet version you get at the local deli. But real coleslaw is quick and simple to make from scratch, not to mention better tasting and better for you. You can add shredded red cabbage or radicchio for additional color.

> 1 small head green cabbage, cored and
>   thinly sliced
> 3 small carrots, peeled and grated
> 1/2 cup mayonnaise, homemade (page 119)
>   or Hellmann's (see Note)
> 1 tablespoon Dijon mustard
> 3 tablespoons balsamic vinegar
> 1 tablespoon sugar
> Juice of 1/2 lemon
> Dash of salt
> Lots of cracked pepper

In a large bowl, combine all the ingredients together.

Note: If using Hellmann's, add 1 to 2 tablespoons extra-virgin olive oil.

Toasted Mustard Seed Slaw

This slaw is served with every sandwich at Café Pongo. One of the most commonly asked questions at the restaurant is "What are those little black seeds in the slaw?" It's asked so frequently that I even put this question on the wait staff quiz. I keep 3 × 5 cards at the café to hand out recipes, and this one gets given out a lot. The toasting of the mustard seeds releases a rich smoky flavor that nothing else provides. This recipe was inspired by Jane's carrot salad (page 205). Maybe you'll be inspired to come up with your own toasted mustard seed recipe.

1 large head red cabbage, cored and
 sliced
1 cup olive oil
3 tablespoons yellow mustard seeds
1 cup walnut pieces (optional)
2/3 cup red wine vinegar
2 tablespoons sugar
2 tablespoons toasted sesame oil
Juice of 1 lemon
Salt and cracked pepper to taste

1. Have the cabbage ready in a large, heat-resistant bowl. In a small skillet, heat ½ cup of the oil with the mustard seeds until the seeds begin to pop. Cover the skillet, reduce the heat a little, and cook until the seeds stop popping and turn *dark brown*. Immediately pour the hot oil and mustard seeds over the cabbage and toss well.

2. In the same skillet, toast the walnuts in the remaining ½ cup oil until golden brown. Pour the hot oil and nuts over the cabbage. Add the remaining ingredients and toss together.

Santa Fe Black Beans

This black bean recipe was served with literally thousands of entrées at my first restaurant, Santa Fe. These beans taste better the next day, or at least after having sat for several hours at room temperature. Be sure to heat them to a boil (165 degrees) before serving. I like these best over perfectly cooked white rice. If you have leftover black beans, try the Sopa Tarasca (page 148).

You can use canned beans, boil raw beans, or soak dried beans overnight and then boil them. At the restaurant, we never have time to soak the beans but still use dried beans because they are much more cost effective. I boil the raw beans with plenty of water until the skins just start to crack. If you can eat one without picking it out of your teeth, they're done. Remember, in most recipes the beans will be cooked again; if you boil them to death, the dish will get mushy. For those particularly concerned with flatulence, you can drain and rinse the beans after they are fully cooked, removing some of the starch that has been released in the water. Canned beans should always be rinsed.

1 large Spanish onion, minced
1 garlic bulb, minced
2 tablespoons olive oil
10 cups cooked black beans, drained and
   rinsed if canned
Enough Burgundy to completely cover the
   beans
2 tablespoons chili powder
2 tablespoons dried oregano, or epazote
   if you can find it
2 tablespoons salt
¼ cup Durkee's red hot sauce
¼ cup balsamic vinegar

1. In a large heavy pot over medium heat, sauté the onion and garlic in the olive oil until translucent.
2. Add all the remaining ingredients except the balsamic vinegar. Stir from the bottom until all the ingredients are well blended. Bring to a slow rolling boil and cook until the beans are an even dark rust color, 30 to 45 minutes. Stir in the vinegar and simmer for 15 more minutes. Serve hot, or let cool in a shallow pan before refrigerating.

Note: Improper food cooling is a very common—and easy—way to spread food-borne illness. Never, with any kind of food (even vegetarian), cover a hot pot and put it in the refrig-

erator, for the center can stay warm for several days, growing bacteria, even if the outside of the pot feels cold. Instead, pour the contents into a shallow pan and allow it to cool until you can feel no warmth on the bottom of the pan with your hand. Then you can transfer it to any size container and store it in the fridge. It's an extra pan to clean but well worth the trouble.

Potatoes au Gratin with Fresh Parsley, Paramo, and Stilton

SERVES 6

These are the perfect accompaniment to a dinner of roast beef and a large watercress salad.

> 4 tablespoons (½ stick) butter
> 6 medium Idaho or Yukon Gold potatoes,
>   peeled and thinly sliced (⅛ inch)
> 1 cup half-and-half or milk
> Salt and cracked pepper to taste
> 2 cups grated Paramo cheese or another
>   mild cheese, such as Fontina
> ½ cup minced fresh parsley
> ½ cup crumbled Stilton, or more to taste

1. Preheat the oven to 350 degrees.
2. Grease a medium-size baking dish or 10-inch cast-iron skillet with a few slices of the butter. Slice the potatoes into a bowl containing the half-and-half, salt, and pepper. This will keep the potatoes from turning brown while you are working.
3. Remove the potatoes from the cream as you lay them in the baking vessel. Cover the bottom of the pan with a layer of potatoes, slightly overlapping the slices. Sprinkle some of the Paramo over the potatoes and dot with some of the butter. Add another layer of potatoes, then Paramo and butter. Repeat this process until the pan is full. Mix the half-and-half with the parsley and pour it over the potatoes. Bake until soft, 30 to 35 minutes. Turn the heat up to 450 degrees and bake another 5 minutes if you like a very crispy top.
4. Remove the potatoes from the oven and sprinkle with the Stilton. The Stilton will soften from the heat of the potatoes. Serve immediately in the baking dish.

SERVES 6

These are the perfect accompaniment for Steak with Caramelized Onions and Merlot Reduction (page 193).

> 6 medium Idaho or Yukon Gold potatoes,
>   peeled and thinly sliced ($1/8$ inch)
> 1 cup heavy cream (go for it on this one!)
> 3 tablespoons dry vermouth
> 1 tablespoon fresh thyme leaves, or
>   1 teaspoon dried thyme
> 2 large cloves garlic, minced
> Salt and cracked pepper to taste
> 2 tablespoons butter
> 3 cups (or more) grated or eight 4-inch-
>   square slices Gruyère or Swiss cheese

1. Preheat the oven to 350 degrees.
2. Slice the potatoes into a dish with the cream, vermouth, thyme, garlic, salt, and pepper. This will keep the potatoes from turning brown while you are working. Grease a 10-inch cast-iron skillet with 1 tablespoon of the butter.
3. Remove the potatoes from the seasoned cream as you lay them in the bottom of the skillet. Cover the bottom of the pan with a layer of potatoes, slightly overlapping the slices. Sprinkle some cheese over the potatoes. Add another layer of potatoes, sprinkle with cheese, and repeat this process until the pan is full. Pour the cream over the potatoes.
4. Grease one side of a piece of aluminum foil with the remaining 1 tablespoon butter in a 10-inch circle. Put the foil greased side down on the potatoes and cover with a heavy weight. (A smaller cast-iron skillet works well.) Bake until the potatoes feel soft but not mushy, 35 to 40 minutes (poke through the foil with the tip of a small knife).
5. Remove the foil and increase the oven heat to 450 degrees. Let the top of the potatoes brown for about 5 minutes. Serve this dish piping hot in the skillet.

Baked Cauliflower and Turnips

This dish is comfort food incarnate. It could be served as a dinner casserole with a huge salad mixed with some bitter greens like escarole or frisée. Or add a glazed ham and you've got Easter dinner.

5 tablespoons butter
3 tablespoons all-purpose flour
4 1/2 cups milk, warmed
3 cups grated Gruyère cheese
2 cloves garlic, minced
Salt and cracked pepper to taste
1 large head (3 1/2 pounds) cauliflower,
   cut into florets, steamed or parboiled
   until al dente
3 baseball-sized turnips, cut into 1/2-inch
   cubes, steamed or parboiled until al
   dente
3 cups fresh bread crumbs or toasted
   coarsely crumbled bread, or 3/4 cup fine
   dry bread crumbs
1/2 cup chopped fresh parsley

1. Preheat the oven to 350 degrees.
2. In a heavy saucepan over medium heat, melt 3 tablespoons of the butter. Whisk in the flour and cook for 2 minutes. Whisk in the milk until smooth. Stirring constantly, slowly sprinkle in the cheese. Add the garlic and season with salt and pepper. (If this looks too thick, you can add a little more milk.)
3. In a 12 × 10-inch baking dish, pour the cheese sauce over the cauliflower and turnips. Cover the top with the bread crumbs tossed together with the parsley. Cut the remaining 2 tablespoons butter into small pieces and dot evenly over the top.
4. Bake for 30 minutes. Increase the oven heat to 450 degrees and bake for 10 minutes longer. Serve hot.

Smoky Southern-Baked Broccoli

I had heard rumors of this dish from my Southern friends but had never tried it myself. For years I was kept waiting for recipes from grandmothers, while my e-mails to restaurants asking for their recipes went unanswered. Things move a little slower in the South I guess. When I could stand it no longer, I made up this dish. I imagined everything that I had been dreaming it to be and put together what you see below.

2 to 3 tablespoons olive oil
10 cups large broccoli florets and sliced
   (1/4-inch) stems (about 2 bunches)
4 cloves garlic, sliced
4 cups milk
4 eggs
1 teaspoon salt
1 teaspoon cracked pepper
2 cups grated Cheddar
2 cups grated smoked Gouda

1. Preheat the oven to 350 degrees.
2. Heat half the olive oil in a wok or large skillet over high heat. Add 2 to 3 cups of the broccoli and a little of the garlic and quickly brown the broccoli. Remove the broccoli to a large bowl and repeat with the remaining oil, garlic, and broccoli in small batches. You are not cooking the broccoli but simply giving it flavor. It should still be raw but with color.
3. Whisk the milk, eggs, salt, and pepper together. In a 12 × 10-inch baking dish, layer the broccoli and cheeses, alternating the layers, starting with broccoli on the bottom and ending with cheese on the top. Pour the egg mixture over the broccoli before you add the last layer of cheese.
4. Bake until set, 30 to 35 minutes. Increase the oven heat to 450 degrees and bake just until the cheese browns, 10 to 15 minutes. Overcooking is the only way this dish can go wrong.

CONDIMENTS
Roasted Red Peppers

These peppers are the basis for many fine dishes and sauces. The same technique can be used on green, yellow, and orange peppers, too.

6 red bell peppers
Extra-virgin olive oil if needed

1. The peppers can be roasted in two ways. The first method is to place the whole peppers right on a gas flame, using a pair of tongs to frequently turn them. The objective is to blacken the skin without burning the flesh. The second method is to rub the peppers with a little olive oil and roast them in a shallow pan in a 500-degree oven, turning once. The second method is better if you have lot of peppers or feel uneasy about cooking over an open flame.

2. While the peppers are still hot, put them in a plastic bag and let them steam. When they are cool enough to handle, rinse the roasted peppers under cold running water, pulling off their stems, rinsing out the seeds, and rubbing off their charred skins (a few flecks of black skin left behind are fine). The peppers are now ready to use in recipes calling for roasted red peppers (there are many in this book).

It is nice to have a jar of homemade roasted red peppers in the house. They keep a long time in oil, and the oil itself adds wonderful flavor to other dishes. (The peppers taste better if they marinate in the oil and garlic at least overnight.) These peppers, paired with fresh basil, are a great winter alternative to tomatoes and basil for a mozzarella salad.

6 red bell peppers, or a combination of
    red, green, and yellow peppers,
    roasted and peeled (page 221)
Enough extra-virgin olive oil to cover the
    peppers
6 cloves garlic, smashed and peeled
Salt and cracked pepper to taste
Fresh mozzarella cheese
Fresh thyme leaves
Good-quality olives
Sliced baguettes

1. Cut the peeled roasted peppers into thin strips and place the strips in a jar. Cover with olive oil, and add the garlic cloves, salt, and pepper. Let stand at least 24 hours. The oil from this jar becomes very flavorful and should be used in cooking.

2. To serve, place a small bowl in the center of a platter and fill the bowl with the peppers and some of their oil. Slice the mozzarella and arrange it around the bowl. Drizzle more of the pepper oil on the cheese. Garnish with the thyme leaves and olives. Use slices of baguette to dip in the oil and carry the cheese and pepper slices to your mouth.

Figs Soaked in Sweet Vermouth with Thyme

I keep a jar of whole dried figs soaking in sweet vermouth in my cupboard at all times. I use these plump little delicacies in many different ways. In addition to being eaten right out of the jar, they can be roasted with beef or chicken. A personal favorite is to heat the figs in their juice, pour them over a slice of toasted pound cake, and top with a scoop of vanilla ice cream. The point is . . . the figs are a good thing to have around.

> 1 1/2 pounds (3 cups well-packed)
>   good-quality dried figs
> 10 thyme sprigs
> 2 cups sweet vermouth or enough to cover
>   the figs

Place the figs and thyme in a clean, dry canning jar or any other jar with a tight-fitting lid. Cover the figs with sweet vermouth. Let sit overnight or longer.

Granny's Sweet Pickles

Hands down, these are *the* best sweet pickles I have ever tasted. The recipe was handed to me by a friend who got it from his grandmother in Mississippi. Miraculously, they are both sweet and sharp and really crisp to boot. Used in chicken or tuna salad, they turn those old workhorses into something special. I like them served as a condiment with grilled fowl or pork; they almost take the place of a chutney in such cases. I also like them with a really good Cheddar and a dark beer for a relaxed appetizer. This list could go on, but I'll stop here.

You could spice these up by adding some hot pepper flakes or dried whole peppers. I think they are perfect the way they are. There are a number of excellent canning guides available; if you are canning for the first time, refer to a guide.

> 7 pounds Kirby cucumbers, unpeeled,
>   washed, and cut into 1/4-inch-thick
>   disks (see Note)
> 2 gallons water
> One 16-ounce bag pickling lime
> 8 cups distilled white vinegar
> 8 cups sugar
> 1 tablespoon salt
> 3 tablespoons whole pickling spices
> 7 to 10 cinnamon sticks
> About 30 whole cloves

1. Soak the cucumber slices overnight in the water mixed with the lime.
2. Drain the pickles and rinse them 3 times. Soak in ice water to cover for 3 hours.
3. In a bowl, mix together the vinegar, sugar, salt, and pickling spices until the sugar is completely dissolved.
4. Drain the pickles and place them in sterilized canning jars. Pour enough of the vinegar mixture into each jar to completely cover the pickles. In each jar insert a stick of cinnamon and several whole cloves. Seal and process in a boiling-water bath. These are best stored in a cool place out of direct sunlight.

Note: I like these pickles a little thicker than your average sweet pickle. Cutting them slightly thicker seems to keep them firmer and crunchier.

Old-Fashioned Applesauce

Very basic and very good. You can purée this with a food mill if you like your applesauce smooth.

> 4 apples, such as Gala, Granny Smith, or
> Macoun, peeled, cored, and cut up
> 1 cup water
> 2 tablespoons maple syrup
> 1/2 teaspoon grated lemon zest
> 1 teaspoon pure vanilla extract

Place all the ingredients in a saucepan over medium heat and cook until the apples are soft and the liquid has cooked away.

Chipotle Sauce

This sauce has many applications. It can be served either hot or cold. We serve it at Pongo as a nonfat, nondairy substitute for olive oil or butter with bread. We also serve it cold with some lemon and horseradish, as a jazzy cocktail sauce with chilled shrimp, or warm as a condiment for grilled meats and fishes.

Be sure after handling any hot pepper not to wipe your eyes or touch any part of your body. Use extreme caution when using the bathroom, particularly the gentlemen. The oil from any hot pepper must be washed off with soap and hot water.

> 1 or 2 whole canned chipotle peppers
> One 28-ounce can whole Italian plum
>   tomatoes, with their juice
> 2 tablespoons honey
> 1 cup loosely packed fresh cilantro with
>   stems
> One 6-ounce can tomato paste

1. Purée the chipotles, tomatoes, and honey in a blender or food processor until evenly mixed.
2. Coarsely chop the cilantro, add it to the blender, and pulse just to mix it in.
3. Pour the sauce into a bowl and whisk in the tomato paste.

Ploughman's Apple Chutney

This recipe comes straight from across the pond. It makes a large quantity of chutney, but do not worry about having it around too long for it improves with age—two months' minimum is recommended. Serve this chutney with a fine sharp Cheddar cheese, digestive biscuits or stone-ground crackers, and a pint of bitters. Think of sunny England. If you are an impatient American (like me), try the quick pineapple chutney on page 139.

If you've never attempted canning before, there are a number of excellent detailed guides.

2 pounds (6 to 8) tart apples and/or
    pears, cored and chopped (remove the
    peels if you have false teeth)
6 pounds (10 to 12 large) tomatoes (red,
    green, yellow, hard, or soft), chopped
    (remove the skins if you are a fusspot)
2 large onions, chopped
2 cups currants or raisins
6 cloves garlic, crushed through a garlic
    press
3 tablespoons minced fresh ginger
6 cups malt, wine, and/or cider vinegar
1 cup packed brown or granulated sugar
1 tablespoon garam masala
2 teaspoons ground cinnamon
1 teaspoon cayenne pepper
Salt and cracked pepper to taste

1. Put all the ingredients in a large heavy pot (it will never be clean again) and simmer for ages. Don't cover it with a lid, as you want it to reduce. Stir with a wooden spoon occasionally. Gradually the vinegar will become thick and sticky. The chutney is ready when the spoon you are stirring with leaves a little pathway. If after about 2 hours there still seems to be too much liquid, spoon some off.

2. When the chutney is ready, ladle it into sterilized pint canning jars. Seal and process in a boiling-water bath for 15 minutes. Store in a cool, dark place for about 2 months before serving (it improves with time).

7

DESSERTS AND COOKIES

*K*eep in mind that baking and cooking are two very different endeavors. Cooking requires an artistic sensibility. One often sees the chef bent over the pot, tasting, adding a pinch of something, then fanning the aroma under his or her nose, then adding a dash of something else. A chef may not even remember all that went into the dish. It was created by tasting and adjusting, tasting and adjusting. This approach would have a disastrous result if applied to baking. A baker takes a scientific approach. Nothing is left to chance. Exact temperatures, humidity levels, mixing times, gluten contents are all factors considered by the baker. Chefs and bakers are, more often than not, as different as "cat people" are from "dog people."

For those committed sweet lovers, dessert sometimes needs to become dinner. When the day has been long and tough, one needs simply a slice of pie or cake and a fork. Or maybe the *entire* pie or cake and a fork. Settle into an oversized chair with coconut cream, caramel apple, blueberry, or anything chocolate. Just let them work their magic.

Most of the next two chapters are recipes created by Cassy Purdy and Mikee Gonella. The chocolate espresso torte recipe was a gift from Susan Purdy to Café Pongo. (Susan is a renowned cookbook writer, as well as Cassy's mom.) The espresso torte was, and still is, Pongo's signature dessert. Special thanks to Rosalind Rhodes, whose "toffee" bars have saved me in many a pinch (when you need something really good really fast).

"Toffee" Bars

The ingredients listed for these cookies do not seem as though they would combine together to taste like toffee. However, these cookies are so rich and buttery that at the very least they should be considered toffee's second cousin. The complex taste does not give away the utter simplicity of this recipe.

> 12 graham crackers
> 1 cup (2 sticks) butter
> 1 cup brown sugar
> 1 cup chopped pecans

1. Preheat the oven to 350 degrees.
2. Arrange the graham crackers on a 15 × 10-inch baking sheet, covering the bottom. Melt the butter with the brown sugar and simmer for 2 minutes. Stir in the pecans. Spread this mixture over the graham crackers.
3. Bake for 20 minutes, then cool completely. Cut along the cracker perforations into bars.

Pongaroons and Variations

Even people who don't like coconut—including me—become instant converts when they taste these delectable blobs. These macaroons store perfectly in tins and are great in Christmas gift boxes. You can assemble boxes of assorted macaroons by making the variations of this recipe.

> 1 pound sweetened flaked coconut
> 1 1/4 cups sweetened condensed milk
>   (not evaporated milk)
> 1 1/2 tablespoons pure almond extract or
>   Grand Marnier
> 2 large egg whites
> Pinch of salt

1. Preheat the oven to 350 degrees. Line a cookie sheet with parchment paper.
2. Mix together the coconut, condensed milk, and almond extract, keeping the coconut as fluffy as possible.
3. Whisk the egg whites and salt until soft peaks form. Fold the egg whites into coconut mixture.
4. Using a soup spoon, scoop the macaroon batter into mounds or balls about the size of a Ping-Pong ball. Place about 1 inch apart on the parchment-lined cookie sheet. The macaroon batter should be handled very gently. Do not squeeze the batter. If your fingers become sticky from sliding the batter off the spoon, dip them in cold water.
5. Bake the macaroons until golden brown, 18 to 20 minutes. Allow the macaroons to cool a bit before removing them, but don't let them sit too long or they will glue themselves to the parchment.

VARIATIONS

Cherries in the Snow

Carefully pit 2 to 2½ dozen fresh cherries, leaving their stems on. Soak them in Grand Marnier, Cognac, or any other booze you fancy overnight. Use just enough liquor to half cover the cherries, and add a little sugar. Cover tightly in plastic wrap and shake the mixture around at least once during the soaking time. (You can use canned sour cherries, or maraschino cherries if you must, but do not add sugar to the maraschinos.) The next day, drain the cherries. Gently, as if you

were making a snowball, form the macaroon batter into a 1-inch ball around each cherry so the stem sticks out of the top. If you use canned cherries, you probably won't have a stem. Bake as directed for Pongaroons.

Jungle-roons

Fold in as much broken-up Heath bar, macadamia nuts, and pecans as your heart desires. Hint: Break up the Heath bars in a plastic bag with a wooden spoon or the bottom of a heavy glass. Bake as directed for Pongaroons.

Chocolate-dip-a-roons

Melt 4 to 6 ounces semisweet chocolate in the top of a double boiler over simmering water. Dip the fully baked and cooled macaroons one at a time in the chocolate and allow the chocolate to set.

Chip Pongaroons

Add semisweet or white chocolate chips to the macaroon batter and bake as directed for Pongaroons.

Seeded Chocolate Chip Cookies

We refer to these as hippie chips. They are basic chocolate chip cookies with sesame, pumpkin, and sunflower seeds thrown in, giving them that health food look. Like gorp, they pack a high-energy wallop.

3/4 cup (1 1/2 sticks) butter, at room
    temperature
1/2 cup packed brown sugar
2 large eggs
3/4 cup all-purpose flour
3/4 teaspoon baking powder
2 teaspoons pure vanilla extract
1 1/2 teaspoons fresh lemon juice
1/4 cup sunflower seeds
1/4 cup sesame seeds
1/4 cup hulled pumpkin seeds
1/4 cup walnuts
1/2 cup chocolate chips

1. Preheat the oven to 375 degrees. Line your cookie sheets with parchment paper.
2. Using an electric mixer, cream together the butter and brown sugar; beat in the eggs one at a time. Add the flour and baking powder and mix well. Add the vanilla, lemon juice, seeds, nuts, and chips and combine.
3. Form the cookies with a spoon, using about 1 heaping teaspoon dough for each cookie, and place the scoops about 2 inches apart on the parchment. Flatten the cookies with your hand. Bake until golden brown, 10 to 12 minutes.

Soho Globs

These cookies are not for kids. They have a lot of chocolate flavor, but they are not terribly sweet. They are otherwise known as buzz cookies.

2½ ounces semisweet chocolate
1½ ounces unsweetened chocolate
3 tablespoons butter
½ cup sugar
2 large eggs
1½ teaspoons instant espresso powder
1 teaspoon pure vanilla extract
1 cup all-purpose flour
¾ teaspoon baking powder
½ teaspoon salt
¼ cup semisweet chocolate chips
¼ cup white chocolate chips
¼ cup pecans
¼ cup walnuts

1. Preheat the oven to 375 degrees. Line your cookie sheets with parchment paper.
2. Melt the semisweet and unsweetened chocolates together with the butter either in the microwave (stirring every 2 minutes or so) or in the top of a double boiler over simmering water.
3. Using an electric mixer, beat the sugar, eggs, and espresso powder until blended. Let the chocolate cool a bit, then slowly add the chocolate mixture and mix until blended. Add the vanilla. Stir or sift the flour, baking powder, and salt together and add to the chocolate mixture. Mix together and check to see that the bottom of the bowl is receiving proper attention. Add the chips and nuts and stir briefly to combine.
4. Using a 3-ounce ice cream scoop, drop the cookie dough about 2 inches apart on the parchment paper. Flatten the mounds with your hand. Bake for 10 to 15 minutes. These can be tricky. They start out dark brown, so color cannot be used to determine doneness. They are done when they just begin to come off the parchment cleanly and they smell wonderful. Avoid overbaking, or the cookies will dry.

Apple Bars

These are a great fall treat; especially with great upstate New York apples. Try a combination of apples, such as Mutsu and Pippin or Granny Smith and Gala. Apple bars are, of course, delicious served warm and à la mode.

DOUGH:

2 cups all-purpose flour
1 cup (2 sticks) butter, at room temperature

1/4 cup powdered sugar
1/4 cup packed brown sugar
1/2 teaspoon salt

FILLING:

4 cups cored, peeled, and sliced cooking apples
1/4 cup packed brown sugar
1 tablespoon all-purpose flour
1/2 teaspoon ground cinnamon

1/4 teaspoon ground nutmeg
1/8 teaspoon ground cloves
1/8 teaspoon ground allspice
1 tablespoon fresh lemon juice
1 teaspoon pure vanilla extract

TOPPING:

1/2 cup (1 stick) butter, melted
1/2 cup packed brown sugar

1 1/2 cups all-purpose flour
1/2 cup rolled oats

FOR THE DOUGH:

1. Preheat the oven to 350°. Butter a 10 × 7-inch baking dish.
2. Mix all the dough ingredients until smooth. Press the dough over the bottom of the baking dish. Bake until just golden brown, 10 to 15 minutes.

FOR THE FILLING:

3. Combine the filling ingredients in a mixing bowl. When the crust comes out of the oven, spread the apple filling on top of it.

FOR THE TOPPING:

4. Combine all the topping ingredients and crumble this mixture over the filling.
5. Bake until the apples are soft when poked with a paring knife, 30 to 40 minutes. Cut into rectangular bars to serve.

Almond Orange-Zest Biscotti

Enjoy with an espresso and an early Fellini film.

2 large eggs
1 large egg yolk
1 teaspoon pure vanilla extract
Grated zest of 3 oranges
2 cups all-purpose flour
1 cup sugar
1 teaspoon baking soda
1 teaspoon salt
1½ cups whole unblanched almonds
1 egg lightly beaten with 1 tablespoon
   water

1. Preheat the oven to 350 degrees. Grease or put parchment paper on your cookie sheet.
2. Whisk together the 2 eggs, 1 egg yolk, the vanilla, and orange zest. Toss together the flour, sugar, baking soda, and salt. Add both mixtures to a mixer bowl and mix until the dough is smooth and stiff. This can take a while as the absolute minimum amount of liquid is used. If you believe it is too, too dry, go ahead and indulge yourself by tossing in water 1 teaspoon at a time. There really is enough liquid; just have patience and a little faith. During this interminable wait, amuse yourself by toasting the almonds until golden and fragrant. Let cool.
3. Add the cooled almonds to the mixer and mix as little as needed to incorporate them into the dough. Purists can mix them in by hand.
4. Divide the dough in half and form each half into a flattened log, about 3 inches wide, ½ to ¾ inch thick, and roughly the length of your cookie sheet. Place the logs on the prepared cookie sheet and paint with the egg wash. Bake until the logs are light brown but still yield slightly when pressed, 35 to 45 minutes.
5. Cool the logs a bit, then cut on a diagonal into ½-inch-thick slices. Lay the slices flat on the cookie sheet and bake for 25 to 30 minutes at the lowest heat your oven has. The objective this time is to drive out any moisture, so they can survive for centuries if needed.

Hazelnut Chip Biscotti

This recipe requires a little less baking time than the preceding orange biscotti.

1¼ cups hazelnuts
2 cups all-purpose flour
1 cup sugar
½ teaspoon baking powder
⅛ teaspoon salt
2 cups semisweet chocolate chips
2 large eggs
1 teaspoon pure vanilla extract
1 teaspoon grated orange zest
1 egg lightly beaten with 1 tablespoon
  water

1. Preheat the oven to 350 degrees. Grease or put parchment paper on your cookie sheet.
2. Toast the hazelnuts in a small baking pan until browned, 5 to 10 minutes. Let the nuts cool until cool enough to handle, then rub them together between your hands to remove any loose skins (a little skin is fine).
3. Mix the flour, sugar, baking powder, salt, and chocolate chips. Mix the 2 eggs, the vanilla, and orange zest in a separate bowl. Combine the two mixtures and mix until a stiff dough forms. Add the cooled hazelnuts to the dough and mix as little as needed to incorporate them.
4. Divide the dough in half. Wet your hands so that they don't stick to the dough and form each half into a 1½-inch-tall log. Brush the logs with the egg wash and place them on the prepared cookie sheet. Bake until golden brown, 30 to 35 minutes.
5. Cool the logs a bit, then cut them on a sharp diagonal into ⅓-inch-thick slices. Lay the slices flat on the cookie sheet and bake for 25 to 30 minutes at the lowest heat your oven has. The objective this time is to drive out any moisture, so they can survive for centuries if needed.

This dessert is so named because as it bakes, the batter "creeps" through the crevices of the berries. Fresh blackberries or raspberries can be used, but they should be simmered first with a little sugar and water to make a light syrup.

> 1/2 cup (1 stick) butter
> 1 cup all-purpose flour
> 1 cup sugar
> 1 teaspoon baking powder
> 1/2 cup milk
> One 16 1/2-ounce can blackberries in light
>   syrup, or 2 cups fresh berries simmered
>   with 1/2 cup water and 1/2 cup sugar

1. Preheat the oven to 375 degrees.
2. Spray a 10-inch-round, 2-inch-deep baking dish with cooking spray. Melt the butter in the dish in the oven. Sift the flour, sugar, and baking powder together into a bowl. Add the milk and mix just until combined. Do not overmix.
3. Heat the blackberries in their syrup to a low simmer. Pour the batter over the melted butter in the baking dish. Do not stir. Pour the hot blackberries over the batter. Do not stir.
4. Bake until the batter creeps to the top of the mixture and forms a brown crust, 40 to 50 minutes. Serve piping hot with cream or ice cream.

SERVES 6

At Pongo, as at any bakery, there is always the question of what to do with stale bread. Good bread pudding is a way to give the illustrious baguette a second chance at glory. What is the key to a really delicious bread pudding? One may argue it is the same key to any good dessert—*fat*. Basically, the more cream and egg yolks in the custard, the richer and more delectable the pudding. Of course, good bread is important, too. Some people like bread pudding made with sliced white bread or challah, but I prefer it made with stale crusty baguettes torn into rough chunks. Customers at Pongo love our bread pudding, with plump golden raisins studding the buttery custard and served warm with foamy steamed milk, for breakfast. Once you learn this recipe, you will never feel guilty about letting a noble baguette go stale.

3/4 cup sugar
1 1/2 teaspoons ground nutmeg
3 large eggs
2 large egg yolks
1 1/2 teaspoons pure vanilla extract

1/2 cup golden raisins
1 quart half-and-half
1 stale 13- to 15-ounce baguette,
    torn into pieces (about 9 cups)
    (see Note)

APRICOT GLAZE:
1 cup apricot jam

1/4 cup water

1. Combine the sugar and nutmeg in a large bowl. Add the eggs and egg yolks and whisk until smooth. Add the vanilla, raisins, and half-and-half and whisk until the sugar is dissolved. Add the bread and let stand for 1 to 2 hours until the bread is thoroughly soaked.
2. Preheat the oven to 350 degrees.
3. Transfer the bread mixture to an 8-inch-square baking dish or 9 × 5-inch loaf pan. Bake until the pudding begins to puff slightly around the edges and brown, 45 to 55 minutes. Poke about with a knife to see that all the liquid has been absorbed. If not, bake for another 5 to 10 minutes.

FOR THE GLAZE:
4. In a small saucepan over medium heat, bring the apricot jam and water slowly to a boil, stirring until the jam is dissolved. Paint, ladle, or spoon onto the bread pudding.

Note: Depending on the size of the scones, 4 to 5 scones (page 256) can be substituted for the baguette.

SERVES 6

I love even the trashy varieties of this dessert that you find at diners and delis. But the real thing below can't be beat.

2/3 cup sugar
2 tablespoons cornstarch
2 tablespoons all-purpose flour
Pinch of salt
2 cups milk
4 large egg yolks
2 tablespoons butter

2 teaspoons pure vanilla extract
One 11-ounce bag sweetened flaked coconut
1 prebaked 8- or 9-inch pie shell (page 244)
1 cup heavy cream, chilled
1 to 4 tablespoons sugar (to taste)

1. Toss ⅔ cup sugar, the cornstarch, flour, and salt together in a bowl. Pour the milk and the egg yolks into a heavy saucepan and whisk until blended. Add the sugar mixture and whisk to ensure that the flour and the cornstarch are dissolved.

2. Take the phone off the hook. Lock the front door.

3. Set the pan over medium heat and whisk slowly but constantly until it heats up, then constantly and diligently until it thickens and begins to create fat, lazy bubbles between passes of the whisk. This will take from 8 to 12 minutes. Do not walk away from the custard because the custard will walk away from you. Do not stop whisking until you remove the pan from the heat. Put in the butter and vanilla and whisk until the butter is melted and combined. Scrape the custard into a bowl and place a piece of plastic wrap directly on its surface. Let cool completely, then refrigerate until chilled.

4. While the custard cools, toast the coconut in a small baking pan in a 400-degree oven until golden brown and fragrant, about 10 minutes (page 54).

5. Mix the coconut with the cooled custard, reserving enough to sprinkle on top. Pour the custard into the prebaked shell. Whip the cream with sugar to taste and mound on the pie. Sprinkle with the remaining coconut.

Life Expectancy of a Cream Pie

Cream pies get soggy—fast. They should be eaten within several hours of their creation, or the same day at least. You can temporarily ward off the soggies by painting the baked empty shell with melted chocolate and allowing it to cool before assembling the pie.

Banana Cream Pie

A classic.

²/₃ cup sugar
2 tablespoons cornstarch
2 tablespoons all-purpose flour
Pinch of salt
2 cups milk
4 large egg yolks
2 tablespoons butter
2 teaspoons pure vanilla extract

FOR WHIPPED CREAM:
1 cup heavy cream, chilled
1 to 4 tablespoons sugar (to taste)

1 prebaked 8- or 9-inch pie shell
   (page 244)
4 to 6 bananas, sliced on the diagonal,
   about ¼ inch thick or a little thinner

1. Toss ⅔ cup sugar, the cornstarch, flour, and salt together in a bowl. Pour the milk and egg yolks into a heavy saucepan and whisk until blended. Add the sugar mixture and whisk to ensure that the flour and cornstarch are dissolved.
2. Take the phone off the hook. Lock the front door.
3. Set the pan over medium heat and whisk slowly but constantly until it heats up, then constantly and diligently until it thickens and begins to create fat, lazy bubbles between passes of the whisk. This will take from 8 to 12 minutes. Do not walk away from the custard and don't stop whisking until you remove the pan from the heat. Put in the butter and vanilla and whisk until the butter is melted and combined. Scrape the custard into a bowl and place a piece of plastic wrap directly on its surface. Let cool completely, then refrigerate until chilled.
4. Whip the heavy cream with sugar to taste. Spread a small amount of the custard in the pie shell and cover with some of the banana slices. Add another layer of custard, then more bananas. Repeat until the supplies are exhausted and the pie is filled. Mound the whipped cream on top of the pie, smoothing or decorating it as you wish.

Note: Chocolate shavings or chopped banana chips are garnish options.

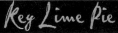
Key Lime Pie

There are many, many recipes for this dessert, and I've tried a lot of them. But I will swear on Hemingway's grave that this recipe beats all other contenders. By all means, use Key limes if they are available.

CRUST:

2 cups graham cracker crumbs
3 tablespoons chopped walnuts
3 tablespoons chopped *salted* peanuts
4 tablespoons (½ stick) butter, melted
1 tablespoon fresh lime juice
1 tablespoon tequilla

FILLING:

2 limes
¾ cup sugar
1 large egg
3 large egg yolks
1½ cans sweetened condensed milk
1 cup fresh lime juice

FOR THE CRUST:

1. Preheat the oven to 400 degrees.
2. Combine the graham cracker crumbs and chopped nuts in a large bowl. Add the melted butter, lime juice, and tequila, adding just enough of the liquid so that the crumbs stick together when squeezed. Press into the bottom and up the sides of a 9-inch pie pan and bake for 5 minutes.

FOR THE FILLING:

3. Reduce the oven heat to 350 degrees.
4. In a bowl, grate the lime zest directly into the sugar, then rub the zest and sugar between your fingers to break up the zest, allowing it to release its magic. Stir in the egg and egg yolks, then the sweetened condensed milk, and mix until thoroughly blended. Stir in the lime juice. Pour the mixture into the crust and bake until set, 50 to 55 minutes. Cool completely before serving. Serve with whipped cream (page 269).

Basic Pie Dough

Mixing pie dough is the second station of the baker's cross. It is Zen activity, and nothing brings me more joy than flaky, buttery, heavenly pie dough. The amount of liquid needed can vary wildly with the seasons, as the flour may be dry or humid depending on the weather. Although it is relatively hard to make pie dough with ice water, the cold temperature is supposed to inhibit gluten development. Actually the extra fat in the milk or half-and-half does a much better job of this. Use half-and-half the first time you make it, then move gradually to milk, then to ice water if the extra fat in the milk scares you. Don't be afraid—I have made incredibly rich pie dough using heavy cream, sometimes with an egg yolk or two mixed in for good measure.

Pie dough get its flakiness from the little pieces of butter melting in the oven and leaving a little flaky layer in their wake. Miserably mealy pie dough is the result of smearing the butter completely into the flour, thus allowing it to melt before it is baked. This also causes the flour to absorb very little liquid, resulting in a pie dough that is both too dry and too wet at the same time.

Everyone has their favorite fillings. The ripest fruit in season lightly sweetened is always best.

2½ cups all-purpose flour, plus extra for rolling
1 teaspoon salt
2 sticks butter (a high-fat baking butter, such as Plugra, works best), cut into very small pieces, very cold or frozen (half butter and half shortening can also be used)
Ice water or very cold half-and-half or milk as needed

1. Put the flour, salt, and butter in a mixer bowl or pulse with a processor and mix until the butter is broken into small pea-sized pieces. Do not mix until it smears together. Remove the bowl from the mixer and add the liquid by hand, little by very little. While adding the liquid, toss the flour mixture with your fingers until the dough begins to hold together. Handle the dough as quickly and as little as possible. Divide the dough in half, pat each half into a disk, wrap in plastic, and refrigerate for at least 1 hour.
2. On a floured surface, roll the pie dough from the center out almost to the

edge, rotating the circle a bit after each roll. Do not roll back and forth as this only serves to develop gluten and ruin your good efforts. Use only enough flour to keep the dough from sticking as you roll. Patch any tears as you go. When I roll out pie dough, it comes out either round or looking like the outline of France or Texas.

FOR PREBAKED PIE SHELLS:

3. Line two 9-inch pie pans with the rolled-out dough. Trim and crimp the edges. Freeze for 20 to 30 minutes.
4. Preheat the oven to 400 degrees.
5. Line the pie shells with aluminum foil and weight with pie weights, pennies, or dried beans. Bake for 10 minutes. Remove the foil with the weights and bake the pie shells until lightly browned, 10 to 15 minutes more. Let cool completely before filling.

Note: If this seems intimidating, try following the Crisco piecrust directions. Don't be afraid to add a little more ice water than they call for. The crust is more foolproof than one made with butter. The taste is quite good, but I wouldn't serve it if Jacques Pépin is coming over for pie (see page 249).

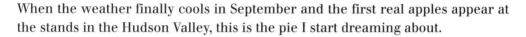
Caramel Apple Pie

When the weather finally cools in September and the first real apples appear at the stands in the Hudson Valley, this is the pie I start dreaming about.

>8 crisp, firm tart apples
>2 teaspoons ground cinnamon
>1/2 teaspoon ground allspice
>1 cup sugar
>1/4 cup water
>3 tablespoons sour cream
>Basic Pie Dough (page 243), made through
>   step 2

1. Preheat the oven to 375 degrees.
2. Peel, core, and slice the apples. Toss the apples with the spices and set aside.
3. Place the sugar and water in a medium saucepan over high heat and stir occasionally until the sugar dissolves. Continue to cook, while stirring, until a medium brown caramel develops. Add the apples and cook, tossing the slices occasionally, until the apples begin to soften and their juice has thinned out the caramel. Let cool completely, then stir in the sour cream.
4. Line a 9-inch pie pan with half the dough rolled into a 12-inch round. Shape the apple mixture into the bottom crust. Roll the second half of the dough into a round large enough to cover the pie. Roll the dough on the rolling pin and unroll it over the apples. Trim and crimp the edges, then cut 4 slashes in the top crust with a paring knife, to allow the steam to escape. Bake until the crust is golden, about 30 minutes. Serve hot, warm, or any temperature in between.

This is a perfect holiday pie. When sliced, it looks as though someone spilled out a jewelry box. The pie has a variety of shapes, textures, and colors that are all beautiful.

> ¹/₄ cup dried cherries
> ¹/₄ cup chopped dried apricots
> ¹/₄ cup golden raisins
> ¹/₄ cup Grand Marnier or Cointreau
> 2 tart, crisp apples
> 2 ripe pears
> Juice of 1 lemon
> 1 cup coarsely chopped fresh cranberries
> Seeds of 1 pomegranate (optional)
> 1 cup boiled, peeled, and chopped
>   chestnuts (8 to 10 chestnuts);
>   see Note, page 212
> ¹/₂ cup chopped walnuts
> ¹/₂ cup packed brown sugar
> 1 tablespoon all-purpose flour
> Basic Pie Dough (page 243), made through
>   step 2
> 2 tablespoons butter
> 1 egg lightly beaten with 1 tablespoon
>   water
> Sugar for sprinkling

1. Preheat the oven to 350 degrees.
2. Place the dried cherries, apricots, and raisins in a small bowl. Pour about ½ cup boiling water over them, add the Grand Marnier, toss well, and set aside. Peel, core, and chop the apples and pears. Toss the chopped fruit with the lemon juice.
3. Measure the cranberries, pomegranate seeds, if using, chestnuts, walnuts, and brown sugar into a large bowl. Add the apples and pears and dried fruit mixture with all their liquid. Mix all these ingredients together.
4. Line a 9-inch pie pan with half the dough rolled into a 12-inch round. Shape the first mixture into the bottom crust. Dot the butter over on top of the filling. Roll the second half of the dough into a round large enough to cover the pie. Trim and crimp the edges. Brush the pie with the egg wash and sprinkle lightly with sugar. Bake until the pie is a deep golden brown, about 35 to 45 minutes.

MAKES 8 LEMON SQUARES

I don't usually like lemon desserts, but I'm in love with Pongo's lemon squares. They are mouthwatering—both sweet and tart, crisp and custardy—a perfect blend of contrasts. The bars are easy enough to make with kids but elegant enough to serve as a flashy dessert (see photo, page 12).

2 cups all-purpose flour
1 cup (2 sticks) butter, at room
   temperature
1/2 cup powdered sugar, plus additional
   for garnish
1/2 teaspoon salt
4 large eggs
2 cups granulated sugar
Grated zest of 1 lemon (see page 53)
1/4 cup fresh lemon juice

1. Preheat the oven to 375 degrees. Butter two 9 × 9-inch baking sheet pans.
2. In a mixer on low speed, combine the flour, butter, powdered sugar, and salt into a smooth dough. Press the dough over the bottom and slightly up the sides of the baking dish. Bake until the dough just starts to turn golden, 15 to 20 minutes.
3. Whisk the eggs, granulated sugar, lemon zest, and lemon juice until well blended. Pour the custard over the prebaked crust and return to the oven. Bake until the custard is set, 20 to 25 minutes.
4. Remove the pan from the oven and let cool completely. Sift powdered sugar over the top and cut into squares to serve.

Note: For a more elegant, individual presentation, you can bake these in tart rings (see page 249). For either shape, candied lemon wheels are the perfect garnish. Boil thin round lemon slices in 1 cup water with ½ cup sugar until they start to turn translucent. After they have cooled, place the fully edible lemon wheels in the center of the lemon squares or tarts.

During the month of August, just outside of Tivoli, Montgomery Place Orchards grows a hybrid grape named Reliance. These grapes are quite rare; they have the flavor of a tart Concord with the ease of a common seedless (read: no workout juggling seeds and thick skin). Don't pass up the opportunity to purchase these delicious beauties. They are wonderful fresh and in baked goods. Don't be afraid to make pies out of these grapes—treat them as you would any other pie fruit. If you cannot find Reliance grapes, don't despair, for Concords can be used. Just cut them in half and remove the seeds.

These tarts have as many variations as there are fruits: Grape with fig and peach with blueberries are two of our favorites. Experiment with variations on the pastry cream as well.

CRUST:
- ¾ cup (1½ sticks) butter (a high-fat baking butter, such as Plugra, works best)
- ⅓ cup powdered sugar
- 1½ cups all-purpose flour
- 1 large egg yolk
- 1 tablespoon heavy cream

PASTRY CREAM:
- 1 cup milk
- 3 large egg yolks
- ½ cup granulated sugar
- 1 tablespoon all-purpose flour
- 1 tablespoon cornstarch
- ½ teaspoon salt
- 1½ teaspoons pure vanilla extract
- 1 tablespoon butter, at room temperature
- 2 to 3 cups Reliance grapes, stemmed
- ½ cup apricot jam mixed with a splash of boiling water for glaze
- Lemon zest curls and chopped pecans for garnish

FOR THE CRUST:

1. Using an electric mixer on low speed, combine the butter and sugar until crumbly. Add half the flour with the egg yolk and mix until crumbly. Add the remaining flour and the cream and mix well. Refrigerate the dough until stiff, about 2 hours. This dough is enough to line about 8 small tart pans or two 10-inch tart pans. You can always freeze the extra dough or bake the extra shells and fill them later.

2. Roll out the dough and mold into individual tart pans or tart bracelets. Trim the edges and refrigerate until chilled. This dough works better than pie dough for blind baking because it does not shrink as much.

3. Preheat the oven to 400 degrees.
4. Bake the tart shells on a baking sheet until golden brown, 12 to 15 minutes.

FOR THE PASTRY CREAM:

5. In a heavy saucepan, whisk the milk and egg yolks together.
6. Mix the sugar, flour, cornstarch, and salt and gradually whisk it into the milk mixture. Set the pan over medium heat and cook, whisking constantly, until the cream has thickened. Do not turn your back.
7. Remove the pastry cream from the heat and whisk in the vanilla and butter. Scrape the pastry cream into a bowl and completely cover the surface of the pastry cream with a piece of plastic wrap. Refrigerate until chilled.

TO FINISH THE TARTS:

8. When ready to serve, divide the pastry cream among the tart shells. Pile on the grapes. Brush the fruit with the apricot glaze and garnish with the lemon zest and pecans. Serve the tarts the same day they are assembled.

Notes: If you have a favorite pie dough you feel more comfortable with, use it instead. To prevent the tart shells from bubbling, simply use pie weights (see page 244). My favorite pie dough recipe is on the back of the Crisco tin. Crisco makes an easy, flaky, dairy-free pie crust. (I always add more ice water than the recipe calls for.) Mikee and Cassy, our bakers, would rather stand in the snow wearing nothing but chef's hats than make a vegetable shortening crust; they insist on a butter crust. However, without their skill and experience, I find butter crusts much more difficult to make flaky.

Tart rings or bracelets are available from Bridge Kitchenware, 214 East 52nd Street, New York, NY 10022; 212/688–4220.

Variations on Pastry Cream

This custard can be modified if you decide to use a different kind of fruit at another time of year. Substitute Amaretto, Frangelico, or Cognac in place of the vanilla and top with anything you like: bananas, apples, pears, and/or nuts. Mikee's favorite variation is to steep Earl Grey tea bags in the hot milk, removing and draining them before adding the egg yolks. This pastry cream is great when blond raspberries are in season.

Chocolate Espresso Torte

This recipe is adapted from Cassy's mother's cookbook, *A Piece of Cake.* To me it is the best flourless chocolate cake on earth. It is surprisingly easy to make and everybody loves it. At Pongo it has become a classic and has attracted an ardent following. I've even used it as a filling between other cake layers in wedding cakes. Foolproof and decadent—what more could you want?

> 4 ounces best-quality semisweet
>   chocolate
> 1 cup (2 sticks) unsalted butter
> ½ cup water
> 2 tablespoons instant espresso powder
> 1 cup sugar
> 4 large eggs
> Whole espresso beans for garnish

1. Preheat the oven to 350 degrees. Line a 9-inch cake pan with plastic wrap (it will not melt).
2. In the microwave or the top of a double boiler over simmering water, melt the chocolate and butter.
3. Heat ½ cup water to a low simmer, add the espresso powder, and stir to dissolve.
4. Using an electric mixer, mix the sugar and eggs until smooth.
5. Add the chocolate mixture and the espresso and mix on the lowest speed until smooth.
6. Pour the batter into the prepared pan and set it in a large baking pan. Put the baking pan in the oven and pour 1 inch hot water into the larger pan (do not allow it to splash into the batter). Bake until the torte is solid but still a little jiggly in the center, 45 to 55 minutes. Let cool completely in the water bath.
7. To unmold the torte, cover the top with an inverted plate and flip the torte onto it. Starting at one edge, hold the plastic wrap and gently pull away the pan. Peel off the plastic. Press espresso beans into the torte in an attractive pattern flush with the surface. Serve at room temperature but not too cold.

Congo Pongo Cheesecake

A classic New York–style cheesecake with a tropical twist. This cake is *rich,* yet fluffy. Be patient: Don't slam the oven door or let the oven get too hot. If you bake it gently, it will not fall. And, remember, all good cheesecakes crack a little.

5 tablespoons butter
Slivered blanched almonds
1 1/2 cups sugar
2 pounds cream cheese
1/4 cup sour cream
4 medium eggs
1 tablespoon pure vanilla extract
3/4 cup milk
1 cup semisweet chocolate chips
1/2 cup almonds, toasted
1/2 cup macadamia nuts, roughly chopped
1/2 cup sweetened flaked coconut,
    toasted (page 54)

1. Preheat the oven to 350 degrees. Cover the outside bottom and outer sides of a 9-inch springform pan with aluminum foil, to prevent leakage. Generously butter the pan and coat the sides with almonds.

2. Allow all the ingredients to warm to room temperature. Cream together the butter and the sugar in the bowl of a mixer. With the mixer running at low speed, add the cream cheese gradually and mix until smooth. Stop the mixer occasionally to scrape down the sides of the bowl and the paddle or beaters.

3. Add the sour cream and mix it in. With the mixer running, add the eggs, one at a time, making sure each has been absorbed before adding the next. Stop occasionally to scrape down the bowl. Add the vanilla and mix it in.

4. Gradually mix in the milk. Add the chips, almonds, and coconut and mix just long enough to distribute them evenly through the batter.

5. Pour the batter into the springform pan. Place the pan in a larger baking pan and pour enough hot water in the larger pan to come halfway up the sides of the springform pan. Bake until only the center of cheesecake is jiggly and the cheesecake has begun to puff and brown slightly, 1½ to 1¾ hours. If the cheesecake begins to brown prematurely, cover with foil. Allow the cheesecake to cool completely, then refrigerate overnight before attempting to unmold. Cut with a knife dipped in hot water.

8

BREADS AND BAKED GOODS

) am not a baker. When Cassy, Pongo's first baker, announced she was leaving, I knew I needed to find someone who thought like a baker. I recruited Mikee, not because he had any expertise in cooking or baking (at the time he had never worked in a kitchen), but because he had a scientific mind, a keen interest in the weather, and a stellar sense of humor. (One needs the first two attributes to be an outstanding baker; one needs a sense of humor to work with me.) The baker is a scientist who precisely measures each ingredient and considers such variables as humidity and yeast cell activity. The baker can describe, step by meticulous step, how he produced every pastry. Mikee, by genetic makeup, is a baker. I knew that Mikee's absurdly intelligent, precise mind could ace baking. With a few lessons from Cassy, he quickly proved me right. Now, seven years later, he keeps things lively with his twisted humor and consistently produces world-class breads and pastries every week at Café Pongo.

MAKES 8 TO 12 BISCUITS

No matter how many trays of hand-rolled breads, tarts, pies, or brioche are lying around, people seem to get the most excited about biscuits. Which are, by the way, the simplest of all baked goods to make. If you follow a few basic rules, you, too, can make outstanding biscuits. On those special days when Mikee decides to make biscuits, the morning staff at Pongo all watch the oven closely. Some even get their butter pats ready in advance, so as not to waste a moment of the right-out-of-the-oven goodness.

2½ cups all-purpose flour
3½ teaspoons baking powder
1 teaspoon kosher salt

½ cup (1 stick) unsalted butter (Plugra high-fat baking butter works best), frozen
1 cup cold whole milk, or a splash more if needed

1. Preheat the oven to 400 degrees. Line a sheet pan with parchment paper or use cooking spray.
2. Place the flour, baking powder, and salt in a mixing bowl. Remove the butter from the freezer and cut it into small pieces. While standing over the mixing bowl, cup some flour in your hand, take a few pieces of the butter, and pat the flour all around the butter. Drop the butter in the bowl. Repeat this process until all the butter is coated with flour. Using the paddle attachment of a standing mixer, mix the butter into the dry ingredients. Do not smear the butter into the flour by overmixing but, rather, mix until the butter is in very small beads in the flour. Turn the mixer off a few times and break up any big pieces with your fingers.
3. Working quickly, pour in the milk and, using your hands, bring the dough together. If it does not hold together, add a splash more milk.
4. Drop the dough onto a floured surface. Using your hands, form the dough into a disk a little less than 1 inch high. Press the sides in as you pat the top down. A rolling pin can be used, but handle the dough as little as possible. Too much handling creates gluten and a less flaky, tougher biscuit. Dip the mouth of a glass in flour and cut out as many biscuits as you can. Gather the scraps, pat, and cut out as many more biscuits as possible. The first-cut biscuits will be much better than the second. (A white wineglass should make a dozen small biscuits.)
5. Lay the biscuits on the cookie sheet and bake until golden brown, 15 to 20 minutes. Serve hot.

Mikee's Corn Bread

When corn bread is good, it is really good; when it's not, it's mattress stuffing. If you don't have time to make your own, the only store-bought mix that is remotely acceptable is Jiffy, in the little blue boxes. Corn bread batter thinned with milk makes stellar pancakes (see Sour Cherry Corn Cakes, page 49).

Ingredients like grated Cheddar (¼ cup) and minced jalapeños (to taste) can be added to lend the corn bread a little extra kick.

> 1 cup all-purpose flour
> ¾ cup coarse yellow cornmeal
> 6 tablespoons sugar
> 2 teaspoons baking powder
> ½ teaspoon salt
> ¾ cup milk
> 1 large egg
> 6 tablespoons melted butter or lard

1. Preheat the oven to 400 degrees.
2. Toss together the flour, cornmeal, sugar, baking powder, and salt in a mixing bowl.
3. Whisk together the milk and egg. Pour the egg mixture and melted butter into the dry ingredients and mix only until blended. Don't overmix.
4. Pour the mixture into an 8-inch-square baking pan or a 9-inch cast-iron skillet. If you heat the skillet before you put the batter in, you'll give the corn bread a nice crust. Bake until light brown, 35 to 45 minutes. Serve warm and think of the South.

Scones are the quintessential British baked good. Flaky, crunchy, buttery, crumbly, like a biscuit, but not. American bakers have bastardized the scone in much the same way we did France's delicious croissant. Now, in coffeehouses and bakeries across the country, we find scones with combinations of ingredients that would make most British people thankful of our independence: jalapeño and Cheddar, or olive and sun-dried tomato. Our scones are still far from the traditional version, and we don't insist that everyone pronounce the word *skahnz* as true connoisseurs do, but we think our scones are delicious, and so do our customers. Scones are great plain and at room temperature with tea, or toasted and gilded with butter.

1³/₄ cups all-purpose flour
1 cup rolled oats
5 tablespoons sugar
1 tablespoon baking powder
7 tablespoons butter, chilled
1 jumbo egg or 2 medium to small eggs
5 tablespoons milk
1 teaspoon pure vanilla extract
¹/₄ cup golden raisins

1. Preheat the oven to 400 degrees.
2. Mix together the flour, oats, sugar, and baking powder, preferably in the bowl of a mixer. Cut the butter into pieces and add to the dry ingredients. Mix until the butter pieces are small but are not completely smeared into the flour. This can be a tough call, as the pieces should be bigger than rice grains but smaller than peas. It is easier to obtain this if the butter has been well chilled; a few minutes in the freezer should suffice.
3. Whisk the egg and milk together, then whisk in the vanilla.
4. Do the following by hand: Toss the raisins with the dry ingredients. Pour about three-quarters of the liquid into the bowl and toss it with the dry ingredients with your fingers. Mix in only enough of the remaining liquid to get the dough to stick together, eliminating any dry or wet areas. Add all the liquid if you need to.
5. Pat the dough into a ball and plop it onto a lightly floured surface. Pat the dough into a disk about 1 inch thick and 7 to 8 inches in diameter. Cut into 6 or 8 wedges. Arrange these artfully on a baking pan and brush with any re-

maining liquid or half-and-half or milk if you have used all the liquid. Bake until light golden brown, 20 to 25 minutes. Serve hot, warm, or at room temperature.

Note: Scones are a lot like pie dough. A proper scone is mixed just enough to hold together. It should crumble easily and totally fall apart if handled roughly. Warning: Mixing scones in the mixer makes triangular hockey pucks that starving dogs will refuse.

Scone Variations

A personal favorite: Replace the raisins with ¾ cup diced fresh Italian plums and 2 tablespoons minced crystallized ginger.

Replace the raisins with 1 cup of almost anything in season—and ripe—to make great scones: tart apples, strawberries, raspberries, blackberries, blueberries, gooseberries. Walnuts, pecans, and—my favorite—toasted hazelnuts can also be added to taste.

Toasted Nuts

To toast nuts, simply pour the amount desired on a baking sheet and toast in a 350-degree oven. Do not walk away! Swirl the pan around when needed to give even browning. This will bring out much of the natural nut flavor.

Sour Cream Coffeecake

When Pongo first started, very early in the morning (or what some people would call very, very late at night) we would experiment with our muffin and coffeecake recipes, trying different fruits, mixtures of flours, crumb toppings, streusels, and nuts. We tried every recipe we could find and decided that the best coffeecakes contain sour cream, as they have a moist crumb and delicate tang. I like to bake this in a decorative bundt pan with a layer of buttery streusel in the middle and a little fruit, such as chopped apple or cranberry, throughout. This cake freezes well for long-term storage but also gets better after a day or two.

CAKE BATTER:
- 1 cup (2 sticks) unsalted butter, at room temperature
- 2 cups sugar
- 4 large eggs
- 4 cups all-purpose flour
- 1 teaspoon baking powder
- 1/2 teaspoon baking soda
- 1 teaspoon salt
- 2 cups sour cream
- 2 teaspoons pure vanilla extract
- 1/2 cup milk

STREUSEL:
- 1/2 cup packed brown sugar
- 1/2 teaspoon ground cinnamon
- 1/2 cup chopped walnuts
- 1 cup chopped apple or cranberries or both (optional)

1. Preheat the oven to 350 degrees. Butter and flour a 10-inch bundt pan.
2. Cream the butter and sugar with an electric mixer until fluffy. Then beat in the eggs one at a time and mix well to combine.
3. Combine the flour, baking powder, baking soda, and salt in a medium bowl.
4. Add the sour cream and vanilla to the butter mixture and mix well. Alternate the dry ingredients and the milk, mixing after each addition until you have a smooth batter.
5. Pour half the batter into the prepared pan. Mix the brown sugar, nuts, and cinnamon for the streusel and sprinkle half of that mixture onto the batter. Sprinkle with the chopped fruit. Poke a spoon into the batter a couple of times to break up any air bubbles, add the remaining batter to the pan, and top with the remaining streusel.
6. Bake on the middle rack of the oven until a toothpick inserted into the cake comes out clean, about 45 minutes. Cool on a rack 15 minutes before unmolding. Cool completely on the rack before slicing.

This savory bread is particularly good due to the moistness of the potato, which combines with the herb flavors that then melt into the olive oil. At Pongo, focaccia is brought to the table with chipotle sauce (page 226). It is also great for making sandwiches. Try it with the spinach melt (page 111).

1 large Idaho potato, about 12
    ounces, quartered and boiled
    until tender enough to mash
2/3 cup potato cooking water
    reserved from boiling the potato,
    cooled to lukewarm
1 medium red onion, diced
1/4 cup good-quality olive oil, plus
    additional for topping
1 teaspoon dried rosemary

1 tablespoon kosher salt, or
    1 teaspoon fine-grain salt
1 teaspoon cracked pepper
5 1/4 cups all-purpose flour (scooped,
    do not pack)
2 packages instant yeast
1/2 cup coarse cornmeal for dusting
    the baking sheets
1 to 2 tablespoons dried thyme
    leaves

1. Place the potato, potato water, onion, olive oil, rosemary, salt, pepper, flour, and yeast in a standing mixer bowl, and using the dough hook, mix until a sticky elastic dough is formed. Resist the temptation to add water if it appears dry at first. If after 2 minutes of mixing it still appears dry, add water 1 tablespoon at a time. Keep in mind that the potato will continue to release moisture as it is mixed.

2. Cover the dough with a slightly damp cloth and let rise until doubled in bulk, about 1½ hours. Make sure you don't put it someplace cold or drafty. The inside of a turned-off oven will work, as long as it has not just been used.

3. Preheat the oven to 375 degrees.

4. Divide the dough into 4 equal pieces. It will be sticky, so work on a heavily floured surface. Flatten out the pieces with your hands.

5. Dust 2 baking sheets with the cornmeal and place the dough rounds on the pans. Cover with damp towels and let rise rise again for 20 minutes.

6. Press your fingers into each focaccia a couple of times. Fill these resulting dimples with olive oil, then sprinkle with the thyme.

7. Bake until golden, about 20 minutes. Serve while still hot or allow to cool for sandwiches.

Baguettes and Variations

When I watch Mikee mixing bread dough, I realize that bread baking may have been among the first scientific experiments, and bakeries the first labs. There are only three primary ingredients in bread—yeast, flour, and water—yet the results can be so drastically different. People have been known to take water from the faucets of really good bread bakeries because they believe that the water, or the pipes that the water comes from, affects the quality of the bread; I think it is something much more subtle than that. Every day Mikee is aware of the temperature and the relative humidity. I watch him squeeze a handful of flour to determine how much moisture it contains. This will determine how much water he will add. The outside temperature will determine if the water used will be warm or iced. In part the quality of the bread is determined by the mixing technique and in part by some obscure magic. Trained bakers can roll dough that Mikee has mixed, but it is always slightly different from his. Other people might not notice the difference, but I can always pick out Mikee's bread. Sometimes I think it must be his hands that make it taste different.

People always think that the foods they grew up eating are the best in the world. They think their grandmother's pie or their mother's pot roast is the best. In my opinion, there is no right or wrong when it comes to taste; I do not believe in a hierarchy of food. A really good hot dog has just as much gastronomic validity as filet mignon. Taking this philosophy into account, I can safely say that Mikee makes the best bread in the world.

1 pound 5 ounces (about 5 cups)
  all-purpose flour (see Note)
2¹/₂ teaspoons salt
Scant ¹/₂ teaspoon instant yeast
  (see Note)

1¹/₃ cups cold water
¹/₂ cup course cornmeal for dusting
  the pan

1. Combine the flour, salt, and yeast in a standing mixer bowl. Using the dough hook and with the mixer running on medium-low speed, slowly pour the water into the bowl. It may appear to be too dry and stiff at first but, fear not, it will eventually come together. As it does, turn the mixer to its lowest speed—we're gonna need some power here! Continue to mix until the dough is smooth and elastic. Do not overmix the dough; try to stop as soon as

the dough has become elastic and smooth (practice will show you exactly when). Put the dough in a large bowl and cover well with plastic wrap.

2. Let the dough rise about 12 hours; overnight works well. Ideally the ambient temperature should be 60 to 70 degrees, but if the ambient temperature is low, you can start with warm water. If the ambient temperature is very hot, you can start with chilled or even ice water.

3. Turn the risen dough out onto a floured surface and divide it in half. Roll each piece into a nice plump sausage, pinch the seam closed, and cover for 5 minutes. Shaping the baguette is the most crucial part of the operation. The "sausage" should be tight and even—in theory it's a lot like rolling up a down sleeping bag from the long side. Roll each baguette an inch longer than the baking sheet (it will shrink back). Try hard to keep it uniform and not like the snake that swallowed an elephant. Take care that the seam remains tightly closed. Place the loaves on a baking sheet dusted with the cornmeal. Cover loosely with a cloth or plastic wrap. Let rise in a warm place for about 1 hour until almost doubled in size.

4. Preheat the oven to 550 degrees if possible (some ovens only go up to 500 degrees).

5. Make 3 or 4 diagonal slashes down each baguette with a very sharp knife (we use razor blades). Misting the bread with water in a spray bottle right after you put it in the oven will help give it that "eggshell" crust. Put the bread into the oven and bake to desired doneness, turning the pan to ensure even cooking. Personally, I like my baguettes dark brown and very crunchy—the bread takes on the most wonderful taste just before the bottom begins to burn—but it's your bread, so take it out when you want.

Note: We recommend King Arthur all-purpose flour and SAF instant yeast; both are sold retail.

Variation

You can also make what we call stuffed breads. Just before the baguette is about to go in the oven, slash it lengthwise and gently part the sides. In the opening put things like tomato wedges, pitted olives, caramelized onions, roasted red peppers, grilled eggplant, whole cloves of garlic in their skins, hot pickled peppers. Drizzle with olive oil and bake. These look great coming out of the oven. Our best-selling stuffed bread is with garlic alone. For these roll the baguette a little thinner and make 4 or 5 deep diagonal slits. Push whole cloves of garlic in their skins into the openings, then splash each slit with olive oil.

Multigrain Walnut Bread

At Pongo, the multigrain bread is the last bread to come out of the ovens and usually the first bread to sell out. It is not uncommon for people to call up and reserve a loaf.

The key ingredient in this bread is the organic seven-grain mixture we buy from a small mill in upstate New York. It consists of roughly equal amounts of cracked wheat, cracked corn grits, cracked barley, cracked rye, steel-cut oats, millet, and flax seed. You can approximate this mixture by buying small amounts of each from the bulk bins at your local health food store.

Once a new sleepy-eyed brunch chef cooked the seven-grain mix by accident instead of the steel-cut oats we usually served for breakfast. The result was a nutty warm cereal. (Using two parts water to one part grain mixture, bring the water to a boil, add the grain mixture, boil for 5 minutes, then let stand tightly covered until all the water is absorbed.) I have been told that grinding your own grain mixtures (in a coffee grinder) is the best breakfast you can have both for energy and health. So this grain mix is not a bad thing to keep around.

$2^{2}/_{3}$ cups all-purpose flour
$1^{1}/_{3}$ cups whole-wheat flour
$^{2}/_{3}$ cup walnut pieces or halves
$^{2}/_{3}$ cup seven-grain mixture
$2^{1}/_{2}$ tablespoons molasses
$1^{1}/_{3}$ cups water
2 teaspoons salt
2 teaspoons instant yeast
$^{1}/_{2}$ cup coarse cornmeal for dusting
    the pan

1. Combine all the ingredients except the cornmeal in a standing mixer bowl. Using a dough hook, mix until the dough is elastic. Cover and let rise until doubled in bulk, about 2 hours.
2. Divide the dough in half and form each half into a round ball. Place on a baking sheet dusted with the cornmeal. Cover loosely with a cloth or plastic wrap and let rise again until almost doubled in size.
3. Preheat the oven to 350 degrees.
4. Slash the loaves in 2 or 3 places and bake until they are golden brown and sound hollow when tapped, 45 to 55 minutes. Let cool completely before slicing.

If I weren't around to slap their hands, I swear that my morning wait staff would have these devoured before 9 A.M., leaving none for the customers who covet them. Mikee bakes them every Saturday and Sunday. If you get to Pongo anytime after 10 A.M., you'll probably miss them. Remember this dough has an overnight rise.

STARTER DOUGH:

½ cup all-purpose flour
2 tablespoons sugar
1½ teaspoons instant yeast
2 tablespoons water

MAIN DOUGH:

1½ cups all-purpose flour
1 teaspoon salt
3 large eggs
1 large egg yolk
1 cup (2 sticks) butter, at room
 temperature

STICKY BUN FILLING:

½ cup packed brown sugar
½ cup maple syrup, plus additional for
 topping the baked buns
½ cup chopped pecans
Ground cinnamon

FOR THE STARTER DOUGH:

1. Combine the flour, sugar, and yeast in a standing mixer bowl. Using a dough hook and with the mixer running, slowly add the water. Mix until the dough is smooth and elastic.

FOR THE MAIN DOUGH:

2. Add the flour, salt, eggs, and egg yolk to the starter dough and mix with the dough hook until the dough is smooth and elastic.

3. Remove the dough from the mixer bowl. Put the butter in the mixer bowl and beat with the paddle until smooth. With the mixer running on medium speed, add the dough in small pieces, mixing several seconds after each addition. When all the dough has been added, it will look a terribly stringy, buttery mess. Fear not and continue to mix. Eventually the butter will be incorporated and the dough will be silky smooth and slippery.

4. Cover with a cloth or plastic wrap and let rise overnight in the refrigerator.
5. The next day, turn the dough out onto a well-floured surface. Roll the dough into a rectangle, roughly 12 × 8 inches and about ¼ inch thick.

FOR THE FILLING:

6. Spread the brown sugar and drizzle the maple syrup over the entire rectangle of dough. Sprinkle with the pecans and dust rather heavily with the cinnamon.
7. Starting from one long edge, roll the dough up into a log and cut it into 12 equal slices. Arrange the slices in a 10 × 8-inch baking dish that is 2 inches deep. Cover with aluminum foil and let rise until almost doubled, about 1 hour.
8. Preheat the oven to 400 degrees.
9. Remove the foil from the pan and bake the buns until golden brown, 30 to 40 minutes. Immediately unmold the buns onto parchment paper or a lightly buttered dish or tray. Drizzle with more maple syrup. Eat as soon as you can without burning your mouth.

Note: The filling amounts can be varied to suit your taste.

9

DRINKS

What can I say? I couldn't leave these out.

SERVES 4

We serve gallons of our maple-sweetened fresh lemonade all year round. The maple syrup adds great flavor and dissolves instantly. For those looking for a more relaxed brunch, we make the lemonade with soda instead of water and add some frozen vodka. This can be made as a frozen drink as well. Make the lemonade with water and freeze it in ice-cube trays. Put the frozen lemonade cubes in a blender with the frozen vodka and whir until slushy.

> Juice of 5 lemons
> ¼ cup pure maple syrup, or more to taste
> Spring water or soda water

Mix the fresh-squeezed lemon juice with the maple syrup. Taste for desired sweetness. Remember not to add too much water. On hot days ice melts fast, so if the lemonade is mixed to perfect tartness before it goes over the ice, it will very quickly become too watery. If you plan ahead, you can double the recipe and make ice cubes out of some of the lemonade.

Pongo Hot Chocolate

Customers always ask for me to prepare their mocha cappuccinos and hot chocolates because rumor has it I make the best. The secret is quite shameful. I use equal parts cream and milk. Hey, it tastes good. If you're trying to be good, however, use all milk, or even skim milk. Try adding coffee or a shot of espresso and topping with homemade whipped cream. Fresh mint, coffee liqueur, candy canes as swizzle sticks, or an animal cracker stuck in the whipped cream are a few amusing ways to accessorize your hot chocolate.

1 cup milk
1 cup half-and-half
1/4 cup unsweetened cocoa powder
1/4 cup good-quality chocolate syrup

3 tablespoons grated Ibarra Mexican chocolate (optional)
Dash of cinnamon
Homemade Whipped Cream (recipe follows) for serving

In a pot over low heat, whisk all the ingredients together and heat until gently simmering. If you have a cappuccino machine, the hot chocolate can be made on the milk steaming nozzle, but put the cocoa in the pot or steaming pitcher first or you and all surrounding surfaces will be dusted with cocoa powder. If you like, serve with whipped cream on top.

Homemade Whipped Cream

MAKES ABOUT 2 CUPS

The orange flavor of the liqueur tastes heavenly in the cream and lends itself to being paired with chocolate, other citrus, apples, and berries. A fine Cognac, such as Remy Martin, can also be used, although the flavor is less versatile. One teaspoon grated orange zest can be substituted for the liqueur.

2 1/2 tablespoons sugar, or more to taste
1 cup heavy cream, chilled
Splash of Grand Marnier

In a mixing bowl, combine the sugar, cream, and liqueur. Stir and taste. More sugar can be added if you prefer it sweeter, but it must be added prior to whipping or it will be gritty. Using your tool of preference—electric beaters, a standing mixer, or your arm and a whisk; whip the cream until it is quite thick. The cream should stay in the center of the whisk when it is done. If you go too far, you'll have sweet butter. (If so, save the solid part to spread on scones.)

SERVES 2

Even for those who are not bourbon fans, this drink might make a few converts. Serve in brandy snifters.

> 10 mint sprigs, plus additional leaves for garnish
> 2 to 4 ounces good-quality Bourbon
> 3 tablespoons sugar
> 3 tablespoons unsweetened cocoa powder
> 3 tablespoons good-quality chocolate syrup
> 1 cup heavy cream, chilled
> 2 cups good, strong, hot coffee

1. In a bar mixing glass (or just a glass), muddle the mint with the bourbon and sugar and let stand.
2. Put the cocoa and chocolate syrup in a mixer bowl and combine them, then add the cream. Using a mixer, whip the cream to stiff peaks.
3. Strain the bourbon into 2 brandy snifters and pour in the coffee. Spoon in as much of the chocolate whipped cream as you can without spilling. Garnish with mint leaves. Use the remaining chocolate whipped cream for your next round or simply grab a spoon.

Note: If you try to add the cocoa powder on top of the cream, it will float. When you turn on the mixer, you will be dusted in cocoa.

METRIC EQUIVALENCIES

Liquid and Dry Measure Equivalencies

CUSTOMARY	METRIC
1/4 TEASPOON	1.25 MILLILITERS
1/2 TEASPOON	2.5 MILLILITERS
1 TEASPOON	5 MILLILITERS
1 TABLESPOON	15 MILLILITERS
1 FLUID OUNCE	30 MILLILITERS
1/4 CUP	60 MILLILITERS
1/3 CUP	80 MILLILITERS
1/2 CUP	120 MILLILITERS
1 CUP	240 MILLILITERS
1 PINT (2 CUPS	480 MILLILITERS
1 QUART (4 CUPS)	960 MILLILITERS (.96 LITER)
1 GALLON (4 QUARTS)	3.84 LITERS
1 OUNCE (BY WEIGHT)	28 GRAMS
1/4 POUND (4 OUNCES)	114 GRAMS
1 POUND (16 OUNCES)	454 GRAMS
2.2 POUNDS	1 KILOGRAM (1000 GRAMS)

Oven-Temperature Equivalencies

DESCRIPTION	°FAHRENHEIT	°CELSIUS
COOL	200	90
VERY SLOW	250	120
SLOW	300–325	150–160
MODERATELY SLOW	325–350	160–180
MODERATE	350–375	180–190
MODERATELY HOT	375–400	190–200
HOT	400–450	200–230
VERY HOT	450–500	230–260